Book Synopsis

FIVEFOLD OPERATIONS VOLUME THREE: Shifting into Fivefold Building provides detailed instruction about building a fivefold vision, e.g. ministry, business, organization. You will learn how the apostle and prophet journey together to direct the fivefold vision. That relationship requires key wisdom tools to have a healthy apostle and prophet covenant. This volume includes directional styles of an apostle and pastor and the differences of fivefold leadership versus traditional pastoral leadership.

And he gave some, apostles; and some, prophets; and some, evangelists; and some, pastors and teachers;" Ephesians 4:11

Learning objectives include:

- Examining the unique applications needed for successful building a fivefold ministry;
- Identifying and navigating through warfare from demonic forces that contend against the vision;
- Being equipped in kingdom knowledge for igniting revival reformation, spiritual infiltration, overtaking worldly and ungodly mountains and systems, and how to establish godly kingdoms through your fivefold vision.

It is indeed the perfect time to build! **SHIFT!**

Kingdomshifterscec@gmail.com

Kingdomshifters.com

Connect with Taquetta via Facebook or YouTube

All rights reserved. This book is protected by the copyright laws of the United States of America. This book may not be reprinted for commercial gain or profit. The use of occasional page copying for personal or group study is permitted and encouraged. Permission will be granted upon request. Copyright 2019 – Kingdom Shifters Ministries

Taquetta's Ministry Bio

Dr. Apostle Taquetta Baker is the founder of Kingdom Shifters Ministries (KSM), Kingdom Shifters Empowerment Church, and Kingdom Wellness Counseling and Mentoring Center.

Credentials

Her expertise to undertake writing instructional books for ministry comes from the following:

- Doctorate in Theological Counseling and Ministry, Rapha Deliverance University
- Master of Science in Community Counseling – Emphasis on Marriage, Children, and Family Counseling, University of Missouri St. Louis
- Bachelor of Science in Psychology, Avila University
- Associate of Arts in Business Administration, Brown Mackie College
- Therapon Belief Therapist Certification, Therapon Institute
- Licensed in liturgical dance, Eagles Dance Institute with Dr. Pamela Hardy
- Ordination as Apostle, Jackie Green Ministries with Dr. Jackie Green
- Board member, New Day Community Ministries, Inc. with Dr. Kathy Williams

Dr. Baker is the author of 31 books and has recorded 2 CD's of prayer decrees.

Vision

Her expertise is built on many years of faithfully serving her local home church before launching Kingdom Shifters Ministries. At her previous church, she served as a prophet, overseer of the altar workers, and a member of the presbytery. She was used as a member of the Prophetic School team and as the visionary to launch the liturgical dance troupe Shekinah Expressions. She has served on multiple missions' trips to various Caribbean nations and has assisted with planting dance ministries in villages and cities throughout Haiti and Jamaica.

Dr. Baker is on a mission to expand the kingdom of God at every opportunity. She has been gifted in the following areas of expertise for helping likeminded kingdom citizens:

- Empowerment, assistance with launching ministries, businesses, and books;
- Mentoring, counseling, and releasing visions;
- Spiritual warfare, prayer, and administrating apostolic mandates;
- Establishing God's kingdom in individuals, ministries, communities, and regions.

Further, she is passionately committed to training others to understand and embrace destiny.

Please connect to Dr. Baker (Taquetta) through kingdomshifters.com or find her on Facebook.

Table of Contents

Building Upon Sound Doctrine 1
Apostolic Versus Pastoral Leadership 14
Directional Drive of The Ministry 25
Apostolic Journey of Apostles & Prophets 28
Kingdom Nuggets for The Office of a Prophet 38
The Ox Anointing: Apostolic Ability to Plow and Build 51
The Nehemiah Anointing 54
Fivefold Revival Reformation 56
Shifting with Times and Seasons 60
Bustin' Out of the Four Walls 68
Taking Mountains 76
Contending Against Principalities and Powers 85
Business & Fivefold Ministry 99
Unique Blueprint of Modern Evangelists 105
Evangelists Working in Fivefold Ministry 109
FIVEFOLD GLORY CHARGE! 111
Resources 112

Foreword

If you have graduated to this third volume, take a moment to applaud yourself and to thank God for your journey! This is the volume that requires a seatbelt. Buckle up and get ready to be permanently shifted to a kingdom mindset. This book will release new levels of authority into your ministry and personal spiritual walk. For individuals who want to learn another culture, they are often given an opportunity for immersion. That means that they spend time within that culture and have no access to their native language or customs. This volume concerning fivefold ministry is an immersion experience. As you read through the chapters, you will be partnered with various members of the Kingdom Shifters team and will walk with them as a prophet, apostle, and other roles of fivefold ministry. Each chapter concludes with opportunity for the reader to reflect on their commitment to their fivefold transition. The content is sensitive to the apprehensions of those who are new to this model of ministry. There is a continual thread of encouragement to address concerns. Any person who is seriously anticipating a shift from the traditional leadership paradigm to fivefold may expect to have lots of questions. It is wisdom to recognize those questions and find affirmation from the team of writers who share their journey with you.

There is an old gospel song that says, "Nobody told me the road would be easy, but I don't believe you brought me this far to leave me." If you are already in a leadership role, then you are familiar with the sacrifices required to pursue excellence. Gather up all your experiences and consider those an investment for your progression into fivefold ministry. It is not just for you, the leader, but to benefit every person God has entrusted to your care. For whatever increase you have already produced, get ready for an exponential surge in your ministry. You are the one who will release the vision to your congregation and to your leadership team. Kingdom Shifters is more than a title to a ministry. It is a lifestyle, and you have just been deputized!

Dr. Kathy Williams, Founder
New Day Community Ministries, Inc.

Foreword

I continue to be honored to write the forewords for these three volumes. **I call Volume 3- The Desert, or the icing on the cake of the three volumes.** In this volume, Dr. Baker allows three of her team vision casters to express in their own chapters: Kingdom Nuggets for the Office of the Prophet: Business and the Fivefold, and Blueprints of Modern Day Evangelists. They were excellent indeed.

Not many authors will highlight other writers in their own publication. Here we see how the fivefold is built from the "Confident and Balanced" main Vision Carrier. Dr. Baker concludes in Volume Three with what I call the desert of Sound Doctrine. After all that she has said and written in previous volumes, she highlights that it must all be covered in "sound doctrine." The final ingredients for shifting into real fivefold building is sound doctrine; *"It is the pure, valid, correct, true, void of error or mistakes, flawless, free of misunderstanding and impurity. Sound doctrine keeps you from sinning."* I have heard many of the main line churches and older church leaders today speak negatively about this generation of Millennials. But I am confident that there are young apostles and fivefold leaders arising today. **There is a remnant of <u>Sound Doctrineers</u> (my new term) on the front lines.** Dr. Baker and those she is raising up are building a sure foundation for the Church of the future.

Apostle Taquetta gave the readers a challenge in this final volume that I want to make sure is highlighted: *"We must shift with the times. You cannot say you are doing fivefold ministry and you reject the advancement of technology, the internet, and other realms of influence that keep the world progressing in being able to reach souls…Get a facebook, twitter, and Instagram page and pursue your remnant and divine connections all over the world."* This spoke to my heart as Dr. Baker and her team for the past seven years that I have been in their midst, have continued to help me shift into technology advancement, as well as dance and new art forms of worship.

Dr. Baker concludes Volume 3 with a challenge to CONTEND AGAINST PRINCIPALITIES AND POWERS. I am so glad she included this as "icing on the cake" for our desert. She reminds us that demonic forces will arise to contend against us and the vision. She says that:

*"Witches and warlocks usually own the airways and spiritual realms of regions. They also own land where their businesses and money operations occur, as well as influence political and economic arenas to instill laws and system that push their agendas in the earthy. As you release your vision, you will be contending against witchcraft that has already been released in your region, as the demonic agents make the witches and warlock aware of you taking your rightful place in the earth. **Remember the enemy loves to hit when we are tired, weary and imbalanced.**"*

Thank you Apostle T... *a daughter and successor of mine, indeed, for your sacrifice and suffering to birth and complete these three Volumes to SHIFT us all!*

"I prophesy that universities, colleges, seminaries and non-traditional ministries too, around the world, will be teaching this curriculum for the advancement of the Church that Jesus Christ is building. It has been neglected doctrine, but Christ Himself will publish it to the nations. Keep on writing!"

Shifting from Glory to Glory,
Bishop Dr Jackie L. Green-Apostle and Overseer
JGM Enternational PrayerLife Institute, Redlands, CA

Building Upon Sound Doctrine

Though no ministry builds exclusively on manmade doctrines, there are godly principles that leadership down through the centuries have agreed upon. Those foundational principles have not weakened through time and are worthwhile to incorporate within our fivefold vision. The intention is always that we are building on sound doctrine and not merely tradition or denominational practices. What constitutes sound doctrine is whether it is built upon Jesus Christ the chief cornerstone. Jesus is the ultimate and major theme throughout the Bible. He is the way the truth and the light and belief of his shed blood, works on the cross, and resurrection restorative power is the only way to salvation and eternal life.

> ***Ephesians 2:20-22*** *Having been built on the foundation of the apostles and prophets, Christ Jesus Himself being the corner stone, in whom the whole building, being fitted together, is growing into a holy temple in the Lord, in whom you also are being built together into a dwelling of God in the Spirit.*
>
> ***John 3:16*** *For God so loved the world that he gave his one and only Son, that whoever believes in him shall not perish but have eternal life.*
>
> ***1Corinthians 15:3-4 English Standard Bible*** *For I delivered to you as of first importance what I also received: that Christ died for our sins in accordance with the Scriptures, 4 that he was buried, that he was raised on the third day in accordance with the Scripture.*
>
> ***John 1:14*** *And the Word became flesh and dwelt among us, and we have seen his glory, glory as of the only Son from the Father, full of grace and truth.*

Though I will highlight some passages in this chapter, the entire Bible is the sound doctrine of Jesus Christ.

> ***Titus 2:1*** *But speak thou the things which become sound doctrine.*

<u>Sound is *hygiaino* in Greek and means:</u>
1. to have sound health, i.e. be well (in body)
2. figuratively, to be uncorrupt (true in doctrine)
3. be in health, (be safe and) sound, be whole, wholesome
4. sound, be in health, safe and sound
5. to be sound, to be well, to be in good health

6. metaph. of Christians whose opinions are free from any mixture of error, of one who keeps the graces and is strong

<u>Doctrine is *didaskalia* in Greek and means:</u>
1. instruction (the function or the information)
2. doctrine, learning, teaching, precepts

The word sound lets us know that the principles and precepts (the doctrine itself) has a voice. It speaks our beliefs and the fruit and source of our beliefs. The sound is clear, solid, grounded, and identifiable.

Doctrine has a voice. It makes a sound!

The sound is healthy and whole. It has no contamination or affliction to it and will not cause ailments or ill will. The sound is not mixed or tainted causing doubt, confusion, or pulling away from God.

The sound is accurate, certain, pure, valid, correct, and true. It is void of error, mistakes, flaw, misunderstanding, or impurity.

Sound means nothing is missing. It is full of God, full of his character, nature, standards, and truth. There are no half-truths, partial standards, and unhealthy or ungodly morals or values.

Purpose of sound doctrine

Sound doctrine will reflect God's heart, intent, and purpose for his written word.

> **Hebrews 4:12** *For the word of God is quick, and powerful, and sharper than any two-edged sword, piercing even to the dividing asunder of soul and spirit, and of the joints and marrow, and is a discerner of the thoughts and intents of the heart.*

Sound doctrine is essential for training, teaching, rebuking, correcting and cultivating holiness, righteousness, right living, one's destiny and calling.

> **2Timothy 3:16-17** *All scripture is given by inspiration of God, and is profitable for doctrine, for reproof, for correction, for instruction in righteousness: That the man of God may be perfect, thoroughly furnished unto all good works.*

Sound doctrine grows the believer in the word, in salvation, and in our walk with God.

> ***1Peter 2:2 The Amplified Bible*** *Like newborn babies you should crave (thirst for, earnestly desire) the pure (unadulterated) spiritual milk, that by it you may be nurtured and grow unto [completed] salvation,*

Sound doctrine guides the believer in the path of the Lord.

> ***Psalms 119:104-106 The Amplified Bible*** *Through Your precepts I get understanding; therefore, I hate every false way. Your word is a lamp to my feet and a light to my path. I have sworn [an oath] and have confirmed it, that I will keep Your righteous ordinances [hearing, receiving, loving, and obeying them].*

> ***Proverbs 6:23*** *For the commandment is a lamp; and the law is light; and reproofs of instruction are the way of life:*

Sound doctrine keeps the believer from sinning.

> ***Psalms 119:8-11 The Amplified Bible*** *I will keep Your statutes; O forsake me not utterly. How shall a young man cleanse his way? By taking heed and keeping watch [on himself] according to Your word [conforming his life to it]. With my whole heart have I sought You, inquiring for and of You and yearning for You; Oh, let me not wander or step aside [either in ignorance or willfully] from Your commandments. Your word have I laid up in my heart, that I might not sin against You.*

> ***1Timothy 1:8-11*** *But we know that the law is good, if a man use it lawfully; Knowing this, that the law is not made for a righteous man, but for the lawless and disobedient, for the ungodly and for sinners, for unholy and profane, for murderers of fathers and murderers of mothers, for manslayers, For whoremongers, for them that defile themselves with mankind, for menstealers, for liars, for perjured persons, and if there be any other thing that is contrary to sound doctrine; According to the glorious gospel of the blessed God, which was committed to my trust.*

Sound doctrine heals and makes whole.

> ***Psalms 19:7*** *The law of the LORD is perfect, converting the soul: the testimony of the LORD is sure, making wise the simple. The law of the LORD is perfect, converting the soul: the testimony of the LORD is sure, making wise the simple.*
> ***James 1:25*** *But whoso looketh into the perfect law of liberty, and continueth therein, he being not a forgetful hearer, but a doer of the work, this man shall be blessed in his deed.*

Sound doctrine helps the believer conquer challenges and demonic forces.

> **Psalms 119:98** *You, through Your commandments, make me wiser than my enemies, for [Your words] are ever before me.*

Sound doctrine provides understanding and steadfastness in the Lord.

> **Psalms 119:29-34 The Amplified Bible** *Remove from me the way of falsehood and unfaithfulness [to You], and graciously impart Your law to me. I have chosen the way of truth and faithfulness; Your ordinances have I set before me. I cleave to Your testimonies; O Lord, put me not to shame! I will [not merely walk, but] run the way of Your commandments, when You give me a heart that is willing. Teach me, O Lord, the way of Your statutes, and I will keep it to the end [steadfastly]. Give me understanding, that I may keep Your law; yes, I will observe it with my whole heart.*

> **Psalms 130:130-131 The Amplified Bible** *The entrance and unfolding of Your words give light; their unfolding gives understanding (discernment and comprehension) to the simple. I opened my mouth and panted [with eager desire], for I longed for Your commandments.*

> **1Timothy 4:13-16 The Amplified Bible** *Till I come, devote yourself to [public and private] reading, to exhortation (preaching and personal appeals), and to teaching and instilling doctrine. Do not neglect the gift which is in you, [that special inward endowment] which was directly imparted to you [by the Holy Spirit] by prophetic utterance when the elders laid their hands upon you [at your ordination]. Practice and cultivate and meditate upon these duties; throw yourself wholly into them [as your ministry], so that your progress may be evident to everybody. Look well to yourself [to your own personality] and to [your] teaching; persevere in these things [hold to them], for by so doing you will save both yourself and those who hear you.*

> **Galatians 1:6-9 English Standard Bible** *I am astonished that you are so quickly deserting the one who called you to live in the grace of Christ and are turning to a different gospel which is really no gospel at all. Evidently some people are throwing you into confusion and are trying to pervert ...*

Sound doctrine helps the believer contend for the faith of the gospel.

> **Philippians 1:27 English Standard Bible** *Only let your manner of life be worthy of the gospel of Christ, so that whether I come and see you or am absent, I may*

> *hear of you that you are standing firm in one spirit, with one mind striving side by side for the faith of the gospel,*
>
> **2Timothy 1:13** *Hold fast the form of sound words, which thou hast heard of me, in faith and love which is in Christ Jesus.*

Sound doctrine helps us to rightly divide the truth of God and his word.

> **2Timothy 2:15** *Study to shew thyself approved unto God, a workman that needeth not to be ashamed, rightly dividing the word of truth.*
>
> **1John 4:1** *Beloved, do not believe every spirit, but test the spirits to see whether they are from God, for many false prophets have gone out into the world.*

Sound doctrine provides foundational truths for the believer. **Titus 1-3** provides an abundance of principles of sound doctrine for a believer. I encourage all leaders and believers to study these chapters and implement these truths into the foundation of your vision.

> **Titus 1:15-16** *Unto the pure all things are pure: but unto them that are defiled and unbelieving is nothing pure; but even their mind and conscience is defiled. They profess that they know God; but in works they deny him, being abominable, and disobedient, and unto every good work reprobate.*
>
> **1Timothy 6:11-16** *But thou, O man of God, flee these things; and follow after righteousness, godliness, faith, love, patience, meekness. Fight the good fight of faith, lay hold on eternal life, whereunto thou art also called, and hast professed a good profession before many witnesses. I give thee charge in the sight of God, who quickeneth all things, and before Christ Jesus, who before Pontius Pilate witnessed a good confession; That thou keep this commandment without spot, unrebukeable, until the appearing of our Lord Jesus Christ: Which in his times he shall shew, who is the blessed and only Potentate, the King of kings, and Lord of lords; Who only hath immortality, dwelling in the light which no man can approach unto; whom no man hath seen, nor can see: to whom be honour and power everlasting. Amen.*
> **John 15:11** *These things I have spoken to you, that my joy may be in you, and that your joy may be full.*
>
> **1John 3:16-18** *Hereby perceive we the love of God, because he laid down his life for us: and we ought to lay down our lives for the brethren. But whoso hath this*

> world's good, and seeth his brother have need, and shutteth up his bowels of compassion from him, how dwelleth the love of God in him?
> My little children, let us not love in word, neither in tongue; but in deed and in truth.

> **Ephesians 2:4-10** But God, who is rich in mercy, for his great love wherewith he loved us, Even when we were dead in sins, hath quickened us together with Christ, (by grace ye are saved;) And hath raised us up together, and made us sit together in heavenly places in Christ Jesus: That in the ages to come he might shew the exceeding riches of his grace in his kindness toward us through Christ Jesus. For by grace are ye saved through faith; and that not of yourselves: it is the gift of God: Not of works, lest any man should boast. For we are his workmanship, created in Christ Jesus unto good works, which God hath before ordained that we should walk in them.

We should not add to or take away from God's word.

> **Revelations 22:18-19** For I testify unto every man that heareth the words of the prophecy of this book, If any man shall add unto these things, God shall add unto him the plagues that are written in this book: And if any man shall take away from the words of the book of this prophecy, God shall take away his part out of the book of life, and out of the holy city, and from the things which are written in this book.

Unsound Doctrine

> **2Timothy 4:3-4** For the time is coming when [people] will not tolerate (endure) sound and wholesome instruction, but, having ears itching [for something pleasing and gratifying], they will gather to themselves one teacher after another to a considerable number, chosen to satisfy their own liking and to foster the errors they hold, And will turn aside from hearing the truth and wander off into myths and man-made fictions.
> **Proverbs 3:5-6** Every word of God proves true; he is a shield to those who take refuge in him. Do not add to his words, lest he rebuke you and you be found a liar.

It is important to note that no one can change or twist God's word to fit personal desire or ideology. God's word is his word. He will evolve with a person in destiny, but his biblical written word remains the same forevermore. Using myself as an example, part of my fivefold ministry vision is to have a Christian night club. Though it is a night club, it cannot have the characteristics of secular clubs. I cannot act like twerking, drinking, and immoral behavior is of God and will be okay just because I put the word Christian on it. The doctrine of the night club still must be in order with sound doctrine, and I am accountable for making sure the behavior of patrons is in line with those laws and standards.

> *Malachi 3:6* For I the Lord do not change; therefore you, O children of Jacob, are not consumed.
>
> *Hebrew 13:8* Jesus Christ the same yesterday, and today, and forever.
>
> *James 1:17* Every good gift and every perfect gift is from above, coming down from the Father of lights with whom there is no variation or shadow due to change.
>
> *Isaiah 40:8* The grass withers, the flower fades, but the word of our God will stand forever.
>
> *Psalms 102:25-27* Of old you laid the foundation of the earth, and the heavens are the work of your hands. They will perish, but you will remain; they will all wear out like a garment. You will change them like a robe, and they will pass away, but you are the same, and your years have no end.
>
> *Psalms 119:89* Forever, O Lord, your word is firmly fixed in the heavens
>
> *Psalms 33:11* The counsel of the Lord stands forever, the plans of his heart to all generations
>
> *Matthew 5:18* For truly, I say to you, until heaven and earth pass away, not an iota, not a dot, will pass from the Law until all is accomplished.

No one change the character and nature of God and what he considers right and holy. Remember, true destiny and fivefold ministry are rooted in the truths of God. God is not going to change because a person or group decides something is not right or decides something should be accepted that God has rejected. God's word and standards have boundaries. When those boundaries are crossed, we have transgressed into our own idolatrous nature. That is what resulted in Lucifer falling from heaven. The mountain that we have created is not the mountain of God but is the mountain of this world or demonic systems. We can claim it is God, but God is not claiming us in return. God calls this *meet for error*.

True destiny is rooted in the truth of God.

Romans 1:21-25 *Because that, when they knew God, they glorified him not as God, neither were thankful; but became vain in their imaginations, and their foolish heart was darkened. Professing themselves to be wise, they became fools, And changed the glory of the uncorruptible God into an image made like to corruptible man, and to birds, and four footed beasts, and creeping things. Wherefore God also gave them up to uncleanness through the lusts of their own hearts, to dishonour their own bodies between themselves: Who changed the truth of God into a lie, and worshipped and served the creature more than the Creator, who is blessed for ever. Amen.*

Verse 28-32 *And even as they did not like to retain God in their knowledge, God gave them over to a reprobate mind, to do those things which are not convenient; Being filled with all unrighteousness, fornication, wickedness, covetousness, maliciousness; full of envy, murder, debate, deceit, malignity; whisperers, Backbiters, haters of God, despiteful, proud, boasters, inventors of evil things, disobedient to parents, Without understanding, covenant breakers, without natural affection, implacable, unmerciful: Who knowing the judgment of God, that they which commit such things are worthy of death, not only do the same, but have pleasure in them that do them.*

Convenient is *kathēko* in Greek and means, "*to reach to, becoming, to reach to, convenient, fit.*" When a person attempts to change God's word to fit their philosophies and desires, they are really stretching his truth, reaching for a truth that does not exist, doing what is convenient, and trying to make the word fit personal will and intentions. The lack of conviction often causes individuals to believe God is with the, but it is possible that God has given them up to a reprobate mind. God says he chasten those he loves so experiencing no conviction should be a fear and not a sign to go ahead and act on desire.

Hebrews 12:5-6 *And ye have forgotten the exhortation which speaketh unto you as unto children, My son, despise not thou the chastening of the Lord, nor faint when thou art rebuked of him: For whom the Lord loveth he chasteneth, and scourgeth every son whom he receiveth.*

God's word does not change. It is not his perfect will but his permissive will that allows individuals to do as they please. Here are some more scriptures on God not changing to fit our conveniences.

> ***Jeremiah 13:22-25*** *And if thou say in thine heart, Wherefore come these things upon me? For the greatness of thine iniquity are thy skirts discovered, and thy heels made bare. Can the Ethiopian change his skin, or the leopard his spots? then may ye also do good, that are accustomed to do evil. Therefore will I scatter them as the stubble that passeth away by the wind of the wilderness. This is thy lot, the portion of thy measures from me, saith the Lord; because thou hast forgotten me, and trusted in falsehood.*

> ***John 10:14*** *I am the good shepherd, and know my sheep, and am known of mine.*

> ***John 10:27-28*** *My sheep hear my voice, and I know them, and they follow me: And I give unto them eternal life; and they shall never perish, neither shall any man pluck them out of my hand.*

Sound Doctrine for A Leader

> ***Titus 1:6-9*** *If any be blameless, the husband of one wife, having faithful children not accused of riot or unruly. For a bishop must be blameless, as the steward of God; not self willed, not soon angry, not given to wine, no striker, not given to filthy lucre; But a lover of hospitality, a lover of good men, sober, just, holy, temperate; Holding fast the faithful word as he hath been taught, that he may be able by sound doctrine both to exhort and to convince the gainsayers.*

<u>Bishop</u> is *episkopos* in Greek and means:
1. a superintendent, i.e. Christian officer in genitive case charge of a (or the) church (literally or figuratively)
2. bishop, overseer a man charged with the duty of seeing that things to be done by others are done rightly, any curator
3. guardian or superintendent, the superintendent, elder, or overseer of a Christian church

Let's consider the guidelines from Titus 1:6-9 as a character checklist for leaders:

	Guard, administrate, oversee, and protect
	Unaccused, unreproveable, irreproachable – blameless
	Loyal to one mate
	Parenting children who are grounded in godly morals and values

	Cannot be arrogant, self-pleasing, self-absorbed, drunken or a drinker
	Must be slow to anger, balanced in temperament, not quarrelsome or prone to conflict, abuse, or fighting
	Not a hustler, sell-our, or yielded to corrupt financial or business deals
	Not receptive to ungodly practices for personal gain, success, or advantage
	Loves to serve guests and good to all people
	Promoter of virtue, goodness, and fond of goodness
	Just, holy, self-controlled, restrained, strong, robust, master of one's life
	Subject and surrendered to the ways of God
	Persevering in the principles of the word, believer in the promises and prophecies of God
	A mature representative of the kingdom of God in life, deed, and speech

2Timothy 4:1-4 *I charge thee therefore before God, and the Lord Jesus Christ, who shall judge the quick and the dead at his appearing and his kingdom; Preach the word; be instant in season, out of season; reprove, rebuke, exhort with all longsuffering and doctrine. For the time will come when they will not endure sound doctrine; but after their own lusts shall they heap to themselves teachers, having itching ears. And they shall turn away their ears from the truth and shall be turned unto fables. But watch thou in all things, endure afflictions, do the work of an evangelist, make full proof of thy ministry.*

John 17:17 *Sanctify them in the truth; your word is truth.*

Ezekiel 3:18 *When I say to the wicked, 'You will surely die,' and you do not warn him or speak out to warn the wicked from his wicked way that he may live, that wicked man shall die in his iniquity, but his blood I will require at your hand.*

Ezekiel 3:20 *Again, When a righteous man doth turn from his righteousness, and commit iniquity, and I lay a stumbling block before him, he shall die: because thou hast not given him warning, he shall die in his sin, and his righteousness which he hath done shall not be remembered; but his blood will I require at thine hand.*

Ezekiel 33:6-8 *But if the watchman see the sword come, and blow not the trumpet, and the people be not warned; if the sword come, and take any person from among them, he is taken away in his iniquity; but his blood will I require at the watchman's hand. So thou, O son of man, I have set thee a watchman unto the house of Israel; therefore thou shalt hear the word at my mouth, and warn them from me. When I say unto the wicked, O wicked man, thou shalt surely die;*

if thou dost not speak to warn the wicked from his way, that wicked man shall die in his iniquity; but his blood will I require at thine hand.

A leader is sound in the ability to watch over souls, speak truth, warn, correct, reprove, rebuke, and empower in love. A leader functions with the understanding that withholding these areas will misalign and can cause death to someone's life. Leaders must make sure they are grounded in sound doctrine as they are responsible for teaching sound doctrine. They are to be examples of sound doctrine, so they correct, warn, and reprove others that are not grounded in the sound principles of God.

To remain sound in doctrine, I would suggest not implementing standards or interpretation that are suspect or that you, as a leader, do not yet have full revelation of concerning doctrine. It may sound good but without clear biblical revelation and understanding, wait until God provides clarity, and SHIFTS understanding. Leaders have plenty of evident sound doctrine to build upon. It is not necessary to go fishing for revelation that does not make sense or lacks concrete biblical substance or evidence. It is okay not to have all the answers and to remain in your realm of knowledge concerning God and his biblical principles. It is all right for a leader to tell their people that they are still developing understanding on particular topics. That level of transparency keeps the leader and the people safe from error. It protects both leader and followers from being led astray and from leading others astray.

Core Beliefs

Sound doctrine enables us to build upon core beliefs that are essential for our fivefold vision sustained in the name and kingdom of Jesus Christ. Our core beliefs must be in line with the word of God so that we can represent, establish, and advance his kingdom correctly and successfully. Core beliefs also provides policies and laws that separates us from the world and demonic systems and enables us to build godly works that represent God. In this day and age where people are being sued for not clearly defining their beliefs, it is essential to have these core beliefs present and available so that when people attempt to get you to honor a policy or law that is contrary to your fivefold vision, you will have these core beliefs in your bylaws to prove that it is your right to operate in the sound doctrine of the Lord. Here is an example of some core beliefs that you may want to add to your policy and laws of your fivefold vision.

1. THE BIBLE...as God's only inspired, unerring and authoritative revelation of Himself to man and is the only infallible rule of faith and practice. (***2Timothy 3:16-17***)

2. ONE GOD...eternally existing in three persons. (The Trinity), God the Father, God the Son and God the Holy Spirit. (***John 1:1-14, John 3:16-17, Genesis 1:1-5***)

3. THE DEITY OF THE LORD JESUS CHRIST…as the only sacrifice for the world and the only way to eternal life. (*Luke 2:7-20, John 3:16*)

4. THE COMPLETE WORK OF REDEMPTION…through Christ's mediatorial work for the redemption of mankind. (*Romans 5:1-11*)

5. THE NEW BIRTH…as the only means of receiving eternal life through faith in Jesus Christ. (*Romans 10:8-10*)

6. DIVINE HEALING…for the total person through the redemptive work of Christ. (*Isaiah 53, James 5:12-16*)

7. BAPTISM IN WATER…by immersion which symbolizes the Christian's identification with Christ in His death, burial and resurrection. (*Romans 6:3-11*)

8. BAPTISM OF THE HOLY SPIRIT…as an endowment of power for all believers. (*Acts 1:8, Ephesians 5:18-20*)

9. SANCTIFICATION…which is the process of spiritual development wrought in a believer's life by the Holy Spirit. (*John 17:17-19, Romans 12:1-2*)

10. ETERNITY…first the righteous unto eternal life and secondly the ungodly to eternal damnation. Hell is a prepared place for Satan and his angels and the unrighteous. Heaven is a prepared place for mankind that accepts God's plan of salvation. (*Revelation 1:8, Luke 12:5, John 14:1-3, Matthew 6:9-10*)

11. THE LORD'S SUPPER or COMMUNION…which is a memorial done in remembrance of Christ's suffering and sacrificial death, and testimony of His imminent return. (*1Corinthians 11:23-24*)

12. THE GIFTS OF THE SPIRIT…which continue to be expressed in the church today and are subject to order prescribed in scripture. (*1Corinthians 12:4-11, Ephesians 4:8-16, Romans 12:6-8*)

13. EQUALITY IN THE BODY OF CHRIST…which is clear in *Galatians 3:28* of gender, class and race equality (both male and female) in operation of offices, gifts and status.

14. THE POWER OF PRAYER…as a lifestyle choice and discipline modeled by our Lord Jesus Christ for express communication with the Father. (*Matthews 6:5-13, Acts 2:42*)

15. SPIRITUAL WARFARE...acknowledging that demonic powers are at work in the world today; a real devil, known as Satan and many names as the ancient foe to the Kingdom of God. (**Ephesians 6:10-17, Corinthians 10:3-5, Revelation 12:7-11**)

16. THE CHURCH...the called-out ones, are the visible body of baptized believers, in which Christ is the Head of His church, and we do support the work of the local church and serve as an extension of the Body of Christ. (**Matthew 16:15-19, Ephesians 1:22-23**)

17. RESPECT FOR CIVIL GOVERNMENT...and the righteous laws of the land. We acknowledge our Christian responsibility to let our light shine in the world and render to the government that which is theirs and praying for those in authority that have rule over us. (**Romans 13, 1Timothy 2:1-4**)

18. CASTING OUT DEVILS...as a major part of the ministry of Christ to set the captives free and as part of the Great Commission and as a sign that follows believers. (**Mark l6:15-18**)

Homework Explorations
1. Journal your thoughts on the importance of sound doctrine as you study this chapter.
2. What reasons is it important for a leader to exemplify a life of sound doctrine?
3. Journal your thoughts about God and his word never changing and the consequences of attempting to change God and his word.
4. Study the book of Titus. Use the revelation you learn to write a standards of sound doctrine for your life and fivefold vision.
5. Write the core beliefs for your fivefold vision with scriptures to back up the policies and laws you choose.

Apostolic Versus Pastoral Leadership

This chapter includes a vital discussion for those SHIFTING from a pastoral to a fivefold ministry paradigm, as apostles and pastoral leadership styles are very different. What you may be used to as a pastor, you will not see in the role of an apostle. This could be challenging for those who are used to some of the traditional qualities and roles a pastor fulfills. Apostles will unapologetically NOT engage in such actions and if you do not understand the leadership style of an apostle, you may become challenged and want to give up on ministry. Don't quit! Remember that we are always growing in grace and developing into more mature leaders. Reading this chapter is not intended as an indictment against those who are currently serving as pastors. It is a search to compare two of the offices listed in fivefold ministry.

APOSTLES	PASTORS
Shepherds the vision and engage with the members through vision and scheduled mentoring of their destiny and calling of the vision.	Shepherds directly over congregational members and groups of people. Engages the vision by directly serving and being available to the discipleship and life needs of the people. Has front-line responsibilities and is typically the public face of a ministry.
Spends a lot of time alone with God and privately administering the vision. Is often social more out of requirement than office and personality.	Spends a respectable amount of time with God and is actively among the people administering and stewarding their lives and the congregation. Is social due to their fivefold office and personality.
Tends to be introvert with some extroverted qualities. Remember that an introvert is one who needs private time for rebalancing and introspection and not necessarily equated to avoiding people.	Tends to be extroverted with some introverted qualities.
May be the overseer of the fivefold vision but not the pastor of the ministry. Apostles who also serve in a pastoral office may be the overseer of the ministry and the vision. Some apostles may serve as a pastor for a season if there is no pastor in their ministry to fulfill the role, or if they are planting a new work.	May be overseer of the ministry but not the overseer of the fivefold vision.

Operates through a New Testament fivefold ministry doctrine that is built on Ephesians 4:11-13.	May operate through religious doctrine and denominational disciplines. May operate through a New Testament fivefold ministry doctrine if connected to a fivefold paradigm.
Is compassionate but tends to be future focused in their solutions.	Is compassionate but tends to be present focused in their solutions.
May plan a service or event but not attend.	Will attend and help facilitate a service or event.
Office of movement and momentum as apostles are sent ones who administer, plant, oversee, stir, plow, build, bring order to a group of people, ministry, organization, or region.	Office is stationary and set to a particular congregation or group of people. Can travel to attend ministry engagements but will return to shepherd the stationary work.
Oversees the pastor and is accountable to the pastor in covenant relationship.	The pastor is submitted, covered, and accountable to the apostle.
Is team focused as this is the foundation of the fivefold ministry.	May have a team but if in religious doctrine, does most of the ministry and shepherding.
May be called to a specific remnant that is called to journey in life with them. May be called to seasonally oversee a group of people to mentor, instruct, and establish a work.	Is generally called to shepherd whoever is a part of the congregation. If the pastor has a specific mentor, they may be called to shepherd a particular remnant and may engage in seasonal pastoring.
Establishes order based on godly character, nature, standards and truth, relative to the fivefold ministry vision, destiny and apostolic calling.	Establishes order based on godly character, nature, standards and truth, relative to discipleship needs, deliverance, healing, and daily life issues.

Let's examine the apostle's leadership style more closely. The following information is from Dr. Taquetta Baker's Book, *"The Apostolic Mantle.*

Apostles are not designed or called to dictate to you, boss you around, or takeover your position or platform. They are gifted with the ability to receive a vision plan and strategy from God on how people, churches, ministries, businesses, organizations, specific works, communities, regions, and nations operate. They also organize, teach, equip, administrate, and oversee others in working that plan and vision, such that they successfully progress in establishing God's will in the earth.

Apostolic Order Produces:
- The character and nature of God
- The will, plan, kingdom, glory, and favor of God
- Power, comfort & instruction of the Holy Spirit
- Alignment/Set order/Straighten the crooked & false
- Balance
- Exposure
- Truth
- Judgment of the unhealthy & the demonic
- Deliverance
- Healing
- Breakthrough
- Freedom
- Healthiness & wellness
- Proper government & rulership
- Establishes the kingdom of God
- Liberty in the Holy Spirit
- Open heavens
- Kingdom empowerment
- Subduing of destiny
- Dominion
- Productivity
- Reproduction
- Consistency
- Sustaining success
- Clear vision to further progress successfully

If you want the will of God in your life, ministry, business, and region, then you must embrace and deem order as a blessing and necessity to your kingdom walk. It is important to accept the office of apostle and to recognize that God has given them the humility to establish order without abusing others or misusing the authority of their role.

> ***Titus 1:5*** *For this cause left I thee in Crete, that thou shouldest set in order the things that are wanting, and ordain elders in every city, as I had appointed thee:*

> ***The Amplified Bible*** *For this reason I left you [behind] in Crete, that you might set right what was defective and finish what was left undone, and that you might appoint elders and set them over the churches (assemblies) in every city as I directed you.*

Apostles are key to identifying and confirming the calling of members and ministries and helping them to seek God for a strategic vision plan to walk successfully in their calling and destiny. In **1Timothy 1**, we see Paul confirming the call on Timothy's life and giving Timothy a clear vision plan so that he may endure warfare and live faithfully to the things of God.

Some apostles have a specific remnant they are to personally mother/father, and/or mentor. Apostles will raise up this remnant so that the future generation can be equipped to carry on the kingdom of God.

Apostles are future focused, generationally focused, and operate in a global mindset. They are about establishing an eternal work that sustains families, generations, communities, regions, and the world at large. The vision plan they receive will produce necessary "now" fruit, while focused on generating multiplied consistent fruit that will sustain until Jesus comes. Notice I said, "necessary now fruit." This is where apostles and other leaders/saints bump heads. The apostle will not be focused on:

- Quick get rich schemes
- Quick hustles
- Feeding the flesh or validating egos
- Fanfare
- Building platforms and high positions
- Filling up pews for the sake of numbers
- Using gimmicks, mixture, or ungodly tactics to flatter or progress

Apostles appear intimidating and serious and though they are typically confident, firm, and forthright, they are also loving and humble. The intimidation and seriousness are due to being innately focused on the things of the Lord and pleasing the Lord. Their heart is not to make another person seem or feel inferior as this is simply a part of their genetic code.

Apostles are mapping out your vision plan and calling while you are walking through day to day challenges. It is not that they are not interested in your issues. They see all of you through the eyes of God and are designed to not only put out fires but make sure the fire never burns again. Their mission is about SHIFTING others into destiny alignment.

Apostles are rooted in the principles and standards of God. They will preach, teach, exude, and live holiness or hell. For this reason, their presentation may offend some and intimidate others, as their lifestyle is used to judge sin and ungodliness. Without opening their mouths, their lives will demonstrate and declare the character, nature, heart, and will of God. Those who are resistant to holiness will be offended or challenged by the existence of the apostle. They will seek to prove that the apostle is not as holy as he or she presents, even to the point of provoking drama and conflict to render the apostle to sin, character flaws, and discrepancies.

Apostles are rooted and grounded in the principles and standards of God.

Apostles operate with a sense of urgency. Their motive is not about controlling others or rushing others into responsibilities. I dare not say apostles will not push you or provoke you, as apostles have an innate urgency to see you be exactly who God designed you to be. To apostles, wasting time is a sin. Apostles are grieved when their time is wasted doing pointless unfruitful, unproductive things. Apostles have such a mandate on their lives that they live as if every second counts. Every opportunity matters. Every experience is important. Every encounter is significant to what they are to be doing in the earth and who God is in the earth realm. So please forgive the apostle if they do not sit around "*shooting the breeze,*" do not engage in the mundane, is easily bored, not entertained by worldliness, not interested in the mediocre, unfruitful, or the temporary, invests in real potential and not perceived potential, always appear to be living in and through their Bible and dialoging with and about Jesus. It is not their heart to negate, overlook, pressure, offend, or cause others to feel inferior. It is their identity and calling to invest in that which is ready for the mantle that is on their lives.

Apostles operate in a spirit of excellence which sometimes borders on perfectionism.

Apostles have an innate drive for:
- Order and alignment
- Neatness/things being in their precise place
- Cleanliness
- Flawlessness
- For achievement and setting a high-performance standard for success
- Excelling at everything they put their hands to

These attributes tend to be accompanied by critical self-evaluations and wanting to please and obey God at all cost. People who work with apostles can find this intimidating and pressuring. Though the apostle is requiring excellence, many tend to feel challenged to achieve the expectations of living by Godly standards of wellness and integrity, especially if they are not ready to rid their lives of sin or enter the process to be fully delivered and healed. This can also be challenging if the apostle has not submitted their perfectionistic quality to God, where it is cultivated into spiritual excellence.

When operating in perfectionism versus a spirit of excellence, the apostle:

- Is striving and working through their own strength rather than the strength of God and the mantle that is on their lives
- Imposes unrealistic demands on self and others that are impossible to obtain
- Create unrealistic standards on themselves because they have no concept of healthy development with time, practice, and study
- Focused on excelling rather than processing with God
- Serve their ambition rather than God's vision
- Place undue pressure upon themselves to perform and excel, which causes stress, burdens, and afflictions
- Mistake unnecessary burdens as the weight of their mantle; they then become bewitched into believing that their will and standards are God's will and standards
- Yield to fear as the apostle thinks God is challenged with them when they do not live up to their self-imposed expectations. It is not God who is challenged with the apostle. It is the apostle's own soul operating against their identity, while succumbing to condemnation, shame and guilt, and inferiority due to not meeting their own unrealistic expectations
- Is being formed in the image of their personal perception of what perfection is, rather than the image of God
- Focuses on running away from failure rather than resting in the place of excellence in God, where success is inevitable
- Aims to attain a false reality of perfection rather than the truth of the mantle and who God created us to be
- Risk destroying the God identity and destiny of others as they are focused on meeting their will and standards rather than God's standards

The Bible does not tell us to be perfect as God is the one that can perfect those things which concerns us (***Psalms 138:8***). The Bible does tell us to operate in a spirit of excellence. It is important for the apostle to know that they do not have to be perfectionistic or strive for perfection as excellence is a part of their nature.

> ***Daniel 5:12*** *Forasmuch as an excellent spirit, and knowledge, and understanding, interpreting of dreams, and shewing of hard sentences, and dissolving of doubts, were found in the same Daniel, whom the king named Belteshazzar: now let Daniel be called, and he will shew the interpretation.*

***Daniel 6:3** This Daniel was preferred above the presidents and princes, because an excellent spirit was in him; and the king thought to set him over the whole realm.*

Excellent is *yatiyr* in Hebrew and means:
1. preeminent; as an adverb, very: — exceeding, excellent
2. pre-eminent (superior, distinguished, towering), surpassing, extreme
3. extraordinary, exceedingly, extremely

Dictionary.com defines *excellent* as:
1. possessing outstanding quality or superior merit; remarkably good
2. Archaic. extraordinary; superior

When apostles operate in excellence, the excellency of God prevails in their lives and calling, in people's lives, families, generations, ministries, businesses, the marketplace, communities, regions, and nations. Just as saints should embrace order, we should embrace the spirit of excellence. Through the spirit of excellence, apostles help saints to operate in and display the heart, character, and nature of God so that people are drawn unto salvation, while wanting to live an eternal walk with him.

Apostles need lots of time with Jesus. Most of them prefer time with Jesus, the presence of the Holy Spirit, their Bible, and with working on the vision and plans Jesus has granted to their hands, as opposed to fellowshipping with people or engaging in mundane things.

Most apostles have a ravenous spirit for Jesus. Often the apostle will feel empty when they are really full. They are insatiable. They continually crave and hunger for the word, will, and presence of Jesus and are always seeking to have more of him. Only the authentic encounters with Jesus can fulfill the apostle. They will be grieved by false encounters, witchcraft encounters, and encounters that do not reveal the full will or breakthrough of Jesus.

Holy Spirit tends to be the best friend of an apostle. This can be difficult to embrace at first as apostles will want tangible supports that can identify with them, understand them, encourage them, and SHIFT continually with them. Though the apostle will have a specified small support system, that support system will sympathize with them and encourage who they are and what they are doing, but there will always be a void that only the Holy Spirit will be able to fill. The apostle will not initially understand that their genetic spiritual makeup is to rely on the Holy Spirit, constantly commune with him, and engage him as their ultimate friend. This is learned as time in Holy Spirit life school becomes the lifestyle of the apostle, and they realize that even as they would want supports and understanding, their greatest joy is getting to know, residing inside, and communing with the Holy Spirit.

Mates, family members, friends, and ministry affiliates will need to respect the nature and character of an apostle. They will have to be okay with Jesus being the head, center, core, and yearning of the apostle's life; and that time with Holy Spirit is essential to the spiritual and natural wealth and health of the apostle. Loved ones must also understand that this does not negate their position in the apostle's life. The apostle needs them and loves them dearly. Their love for God does not replace their love for them.

The apostle will have to be cognizant of the needs and desires of their mates, family members, friends, and ministry affiliates. They will have to be effective - consistent communicators, and heart felt expressers of their love, devotion, and appreciation for those in their life. Despite not having a love for the mundane, the apostle will have to allow their love for their marriage, family, friends, etc., empower them to take time to nurture, cultivate, and strengthen relationships, and to even view this as important to God for their life.

I will state that regardless to how much time the apostle spends with family and friends, because of the call upon the apostle's life and the need for communing with the Holy Spirit, there is a huge sacrifice regarding time and relationships, that the apostle and his or her loved ones have to endure. The calling of the apostle costs and I am not sure there is any way around that. I do know that Jesus himself said that a hundredfold return will come to those who sacrifice in this nature. I therefore, hold on to that and pray that my family and friends can love me through my calling, and respect that Jesus will bless us for all the sacrifices we endeavor for him and his kingdom.

> ***Mark 10:29-31*** *Then Peter began to say unto him, Lo, we have left all, and have followed thee. And Jesus answered and said, Verily I say unto you, There is no man that hath left house, or brethren, or sisters, or father, or mother, or wife, or children, or lands, for my sake, and the gospel's, But he shall receive an hundredfold now in this time, houses, and brethren, and sisters, and mothers, and children, and lands, with persecutions; and in the world to come eternal life. But many that are first shall be last; and the last first.*

Apostles experience seasons of loneliness and isolation. This can and may very well be abandonment as some will leave for legitimate reasons, some leave because it is God's design, some will leave for ill-advised reasons, and some will leave for no apparent reason at all. Sometimes having to spend time with the Holy Spirit can in and of itself, cause loneliness and abandonment. People feel unappreciated and ostracized by the apostle's time with the Holy Spirit so they leave, or they may not understand the call and requirements of an apostle, so they leave. Some just simply cannot go where God is taking the apostle so the isolation with the Holy Spirit causes a separation. Though the ministry, community, or business endeavors can be full of people or the home of an apostle can be full of family, the apostle can still experience loneliness and isolation. The apostle is often years ahead of those around them, so while others are engaged in the present vision, they are with God working on visions that are ten to twenty years into the future. This can be lonely and boring when the apostle is not able to share what God is speaking or if those around them are not ready to hear or engage in future visions. The apostle has to practice finding joy in watching others blossom and in seeing visions unfold in the present, even when they have already lived the vision in their spirit walk with the Lord. Sometimes the apostle has to practice relearning subjects they have already been taught with the Holy Spirit so they can be engaged in the present vision and in the present learning of those around them.

This can be humbling as the apostle has to submit themselves to journeying where the people are, while continuing to live and journey in spiritual dimensions with the Holy Spirit. The enemy loves to make apostles feel like they are all alone and no one understands or can journey with them. When the apostle understands that isolation and loneliness is a part of their kingdom walk, they will avoid challenges with depression and woundedness that comes from having to spend seasons alone. They will also avoid becoming angry, offended, and resentful of people and loved ones who cannot go where they are in God for that season, do not understand it, or become challenged by it.

Speaking of dimensions, apostles experience constant SHIFTS in God. They go from level to level, glory to glory, dimension to dimension continually. Sometimes this can be overwhelming, feel like a roller coaster or race, but most times it is adventurous and fun. Levels are like going to the next street over. Dimensions are like going to the next town – state over. Levels feel like you are elevating in God, while dimensions often feel like you are blasting off like a rocket concerning the things of God. Apostles usually feel as if they are always spiritually treading, towering, and running in the spirit realm, even as they are taking up territory in the natural realm.

The apostle may as well experience a continual pressing upward as they go from levels or dimensions with God. This pressing feels like a constant perseverance, and as the apostle presses, there is a pressing on every side that tends to occur against the apostle.

> **2Corinthians 3:18** *But we all, with open face beholding as in a glass the glory of the Lord, are changed into the same image from glory to glory, even as by the Spirit of the Lord.*

> ***Philippians 3:14*** *I press toward the mark for the prize of the high calling of God in Christ Jesus.*
>
> ***1Corinthians 9:24*** *Know ye not that they which run in a race run all, but one receiveth the prize? So run, that ye may obtain.*
>
> ***2Corinthians 4:8*** *We are troubled on every side, yet not distressed; we are perplexed, but not in despair.*

Apostles have the ability to overcome the greatest of adversities. Though they are constantly faced with severe trials, tribulations, and death, they tend to defy every odd. Their lives are in the hands of God, and he uses near death experiences as testimonies of his supernatural power and protection that surrounds the apostle, and how the representation of Jesus is evident upon them.

> ***2Corinthians 4:9-12 The Amplified Bible*** *We are pursued (persecuted and hard driven), but not deserted [to stand alone]; we are struck down to the ground, but never struck out and destroyed; Always carrying about in the body the liability and exposure to the same putting to death that the Lord Jesus suffered, so that the [resurrection] life of Jesus also may be shown forth by and in our bodies.*
>
> *For we who live are constantly [experiencing] being handed over to death for Jesus' sake, that the [resurrection] life of Jesus also may be evidenced through our flesh which is liable to death. Thus death is actively at work in us, but [it is in order that our] life [may be actively at work] in you.*

Apostles glory in persevering. They enjoy bragging on God and being able to demonstrate the overcoming power of God.

Homework Explorations
1. Journal what you learned regarding the differences between the leadership role of an apostle and a pastor.
2. Journal your thoughts regarding the leadership style of an apostle.
3. As you consider your experience, personality, and identity, what challenges and successes you believe you would have with an apostle as an overseer. Journal this in detail.

4. Write a one page paper on an apostle that you have come in contact with. Journal their personality type and leadership style as it relates to this chapter. Journal your experience with them and any way this chapter could have helped you with the relationship interactions.

Directional Drive of The Ministry

Apostles and Prophets are offices that help drive and guide the momentum of fivefold ministry, and the people, ministries, lands, atmospheres, regions and spheres they operate in. They seek words, strategies and revelations to steer the ministry in the direction and kingdom advancement of the Lord. If apostles and prophets are not properly aligned to see vision and hear from God, the vision can be stifled and even die. If they become contaminated, the ministry vision can become impure, be altered, and exposed to the enemy. If they become complacent, the ministry vision can stagnate and even SHIFT back into old paradigms.

Apostles are visionaries.
Prophets are the mouthpiece of God.

The vision of fivefold is a movement and not an isolated mission. In **John 4:20-24**, Jesus tells the Samaritan woman that it was not about what mountain she worshipped on, but that she worshiped in spirit and in truth.

> *Our fathers worshipped in this mountain; and ye say, that in Jerusalem is the place where men ought to worship. Jesus saith unto her, Woman, believe me, the hour cometh, when ye shall neither in this mountain, nor yet at Jerusalem, worship the Father. Ye worship ye know not what: we know what we worship: for salvation is of the Jews. But the hour cometh, and now is, when the true worshippers shall worship the Father in spirit and in truth: for the Father seeketh such to worship him. God is a Spirit: and they that worship him must worship him in spirit and in truth.*

It is important to note that:
- ❖ We are not bound by tradition or religion.
- ❖ What worked or did not work yesterday.
- ❖ What our ancestors did or did not do.
- ❖ What was established or considered the appropriate way to experience and live in God.

Fivefold ministry is about living a daily lifestyle of spiritual covenant worship and relationship with the Lord. We live in momentum with him as he drives the destiny and calling upon our lives. This is essential for the apostle and the prophet who has to make sure the people, the ministry, and the region keeps SHIFTING and moving with God.

One of the ways my ministry remain mobile with God is through the prophets. I continuously seek God for prophetic words, revelations, and strategies concerning the members, the ministry vision, the body of Christ, the region, and our sphere of influence.

- We utilize this information as God leads.
- We do not build high places (stagnant strategy) so as God reveals and change strategies and directions, so do we.
- We respect the momentum of others but do not compare ourselves to others. We implement what works for us, resist inserting tactics that he did not say, while trusting him with our results.
- We remain in our Metron (realm of influence); if we do not have the manpower or authority for a particular jurisdiction, we do not drive into these territories. This is vital as people will discern your potential and will relent all type self-imposed ideas that are not in alignment with the vision God has provided. We work our Metron by seeking to please God not man.

As we work the revelations and insights God gives, prayer, empowerment, and fellowship are constant foundational spiritual endeavors we engage in.

My team and I pray together into the information two to three times a week. Please understand that everything regarding the vision is birthed, cultivated, built, and advanced in prayer. Apostles and prophets are gatekeepers and watchmen of the vision, They are scouting the walls and guarding the gates in spiritual realms - making sure the vision is safe and flourishing as God intends.

> *Isaiah 62:6 On your walls, O Jerusalem, I have appointed watchmen; All day and all night they will never keep silent You who remind the LORD, take no rest for yourselves.*
>
> *Isaiah 66:9 Shall I bring to the birth, and not cause to bring forth? saith the LORD: shall I cause to bring forth, and shut the womb? saith thy God.*
>
> *Habakkuk 2:1 I will stand on my guard post And station myself on the rampart; And I will keep watch to see what He will speak to me, And how I may reply when I am reproved.*
>
> *John 3:6 That which is born of the flesh is flesh, and that which is born of the Spirit is spirit.*

Philippians 4:6 *Do not be anxious about anything, but in everything, by prayer and petition, with thanksgiving, present your requests to God.*

Jeremiah 29:12 *Then you will call on me and come and pray to me, and I will listen to you.*

Jeremiah 33:3 *Call to me and I will answer you and tell you great and unsearchable things you do not know.*

Mark 11:24 *Therefore I tell you, whatever you ask for in prayer, believe that you have received it, and it will be yours.*

Jesus empowered the Samaritan woman and encouraged her to journey in the new paradigm he was revealing to her. My team and I consistently empower one another to live for God and to adhere to the strategies and insights he releases. As we encourage one another to trust God, we create a culture to unwavering faith in kingdom vision and existing in destiny as a lifestyle. Plan Bs are fleeting to nonexistent as we lean on one another for support in working what God has granted to our hands. Each team member recognizes that they are not alone and are esteemed.

Homework Explorations
1. How does the apostle and prophet work together to drive the vision of the fivefold ministry.
2. What reasons is prayer essential for birthing, building, and advancing the fivefold ministry.
3. What reasons is it important for apostles and prophets to pray together?
4. What reasons is it important for apostles and prophets to seek godly revelation to guide the ministry.
5. Journal how an apostle and prophet relationship look in your fivefold ministry.

Apostolic Journey of Apostles & Prophets

By: Prophet Dana Wade, Vision Carrier of Kingdom Shifters Ministries Virginia

There has always been a unique relationship between apostles and prophets as foundational gifts to the building of the church. Did the original apostles and prophets lay the foundation? Yes, but these ascension gifts are still needed in the expansion and building process in each person's life and generation until the return of Christ.

> ***Ephesians 4:11-13*** *So Christ himself gave the apostles, the prophets, the evangelists, the pastors and teachers, to equip his people for works of service, so that the body of Christ may be built up until we all reach unity in the faith and in the knowledge of the Son of God and become mature, attaining to the whole measure of the fullness of Christ.*

We are the temple of the Holy Ghost and Christ is building us up into the full measure and stature of himself until we reach the unity of the faith and full measure of the fullness of Christ. He does this through the five grace, ascension gifts, two of which are apostle and prophet.

All of the five-fold offices are meant to work together as a team, but there is a unique relationship between apostles and prophets, as governors and high-ranking officers in the spirit. Apostles and prophets are tasked with gatekeeping and the displacement of principalities and ruling spirits in regions and territories. They are mandated uniquely to equip the saints in matters of spiritual warfare, identity and calling, so everyone is walking in destiny. The roles, functions and responsibilities of the evangelist, pastor and teacher differ from that of apostles and prophets. Not better mind you, just different. Those three gifts are tasked more with rescuing the lost and ministering to those in need while, prophets and apostles administrate the kingdom on earth.

As a prophet, my life is the message. – Prophet Dana Wade

As apostles and prophets endeavor to work together their shared interest and goal of establishing the kingdom on earth is what propels them in focus and like fashion. Their roles and responsibilities are different, but when they are combined, they produce a powerful, multiplying affect in prayer, intercession, warfare and in service to others.

I remember when I realized what had been missing in my life as a prophet, after having my first interaction in prayer and conversation with Apostle Taquetta Baker. I experienced God in a whole new way as we prayed together. I experienced clarity, and authority in the spirit as we prayed together and soared higher. Plus, I had language and clarity in prayer that I previously did not. As a prophet, my life is the message- I am the Word of God in the earth; I need an apostle to give language and definition to what I am experiencing and living out on a daily basis, especially in prayer. The Bible says in *John 1:14* "The Word became flesh and made his dwelling among us." This is the life of a prophet, as our lives and very existence is the Word of God being made manifested in the earth in fleshly form. As we understand that prophets are the living word, we understand that apostles bring the clarity, focus, insight, definition and expression to the word that God is revealing though the life of the prophet.

The more Taquetta and I talked week after week, month after month, the more the kingdom and my prophetic office was being established. The spiritual heavenlies were opened and I was experiencing a wonderful dimension of fullness in the spirit. As a prophet, I live to hear the voice of God, and see into the spirit realm as to reveal the heart and mind of God, so this new openness and clarity changed everything for me, as she naturally operated as an apostle with me.

I remember talking with Apostle Taquetta and saying yes, yes, yes on so many different occasions. Why you may ask? Because she was bringing the clarity that I had been missing for years. She SHIFTED me in every conversation out of the old paradigm of being prophetic into my office as a prophet. I knew how to be prophetic, and I knew I was a prophet; but I did not have the fullness of it, and apostles carry more of the fullness that prophets need. I knew my life was the message, but she was able to explain all of it on a deeper level. I then began to embody my office, not just know about it. Prophets will see, hear and reveal, but apostles clarify, define and build upon the revelation that is given. Much of what I experience as a prophet is symbolic, as I have dreams and encounters that need interpretation, so I must discern on a higher level, and apostles help prophets with this.

Apostles carry a greater dimension of glory. – Prophet Dana Wade

It cannot be understated that apostles carry a greater dimension of glory, so we must stay connected in covenant relationship. Covenant relationships originate with God and are centered in his will with his divine plans and purposes as the focus for the relationship. Covenants must be taken seriously and must have definitive roles, to complete the intentions of God in the earth. The covenants between apostles and prophets must be stewarded thoughtfully and carefully, as they are called to closely govern alongside one another, establishing God's kingdom on earth. Apostolic and prophetic covenants carry a flow and dimension of glory that is needed to sustain a vision and the relationship is different for that reason. GLORY MATTERS - it is the essence of God and it is the way we experience "the more of God." Within the glory is the realm of miracles, signs and wonders, increase, multiplication, healing, deliverance and all of who God is. For so many years I felt so incomplete as a prophet, because I did not have that connection of glory. I had plenty of revelation, but I lacked the clarity, glory, wisdom and understanding that was needed to implement things, and advance me further into destiny. One of the key areas of wisdom I gained was in prayer. I learned to pray differently, as I now was SHIFTING higher into my seat of authority as prophet. I learned the concept of team prayer as team prayer is a building prayer, which takes the effort of everyone involved. Apostles help prophets advance in destiny and better understand how to implement their role in administering the kingdom on the earth. Now mind you, not all prophets and apostles are created equal, because we are all maturing and coming into our calling.   However, this has been my experience with Apostle Taquetta, as her maturation process has been years in the making.

The flow of glory that apostles carry is immense and is no joke. It is vital in the growth and development of prophets, so they can experience and embody their office and seat of authority. This flow of glory cannot be underestimated for the prophet because it is the source and life-flow of God through the apostle. Prophets need that flow to ground them because apostles bring prophets back to earth from all their soaring in the heavenlies, grounding them in the true wealth of the word and the necessity of building and releasing his kingdom to others. If apostles are not connected to prophets, then the kingdom is not being demonstrated and established in the territories and regions they live in.

The offices of the apostle and prophet are a huge part of the reformation that is taking place now within the Body of Christ, as they are foundational to building the kingdom. The world needs the apostle and the prophet working together with all the other five-fold ministers. It has been a terribly missed element of experiencing God and building the kingdom in the earth. I believe God is honoring the apostle and prophet in the earth, once again because it is two of the most powerful ways we know and experience who God is. Jesus was the greatest apostle and prophet ever, and without this expression of him being represented in the earth, we miss a most powerful facet of God. The office of the apostle is one of power in signs, miracles and wonders and the office of the prophet is one who reveals and represents the word and embodiment of Jesus. So, their combined uniqueness brings the voice, life, expression and power of Jesus in the earth, as they minister in each region. Remember Jesus said, "I'll never leave you nor forsake you" and he does this as he ministers through the apostle and prophet, by the power and life of Holy Spirit within them, wherever they go.

The Apostle & Prophet Relationship Operation

> **Acts 5:12** *"The apostles performed many signs and wonders among the people."*

> **Acts 13:1-2** *"Now in the church at Antioch there were prophets and teachers: Barnabas, Simeon called Niger, Lucius of Cyrene, Manaen (who had been brought up with Herod the tetrarch) and Saul. While they were worshiping the Lord and fasting, the Holy Spirit said, "Set apart for me Barnabas and Saul for the work to which I have called them." So after they had fasted and prayed, they placed their hands on them and sent them off."*

In the above scripture we see Saul, soon to be Apostle Paul, and Barnabas the prophet, being set apart and sent by the Holy Spirit for the work of the ministry. Apostles are sent ones, meant to show forth the presence and power of God and prophets are the embodiment of the Word being sent, as Jesus in the earth.

And in the scripture below we see the result of the two ascension gifts working together:

> **Acts 13:4-12** *"The two of them, sent on their way by the Holy Spirit, went down to Seleucia and sailed from there to Cyprus. When they arrived at Salamis, they proclaimed the word of God in the Jewish synagogues. John was with them as their helper. They traveled through the whole island until they came to Paphos. There they met a Jewish sorcerer and false prophet named Bar-Jesus, who was an attendant of the proconsul, Sergius Paulus. The proconsul, an intelligent man, sent for Barnabas and Saul because he wanted to hear the word of God. But Elymas the sorcerer (for that is what his name means) opposed them and tried to turn the proconsul from the faith. Then Saul, who was also called Paul, filled with the Holy Spirit, looked straight at Elymas and said, "You are a child of the devil and an enemy of everything that is right! You are full of all kinds of deceit and trickery. Will you never stop perverting the right ways of the Lord? Now the hand of the Lord is against you. You are going to be blind for a time, not even able to see the light of the sun." Immediately mist and darkness came over him, and he groped about, seeking someone to lead him by the hand. When the proconsul saw what had happened, he believed, for he was amazed at the teaching about the Lord."*

As Saul the apostle and Barnabas the prophet worked closely together going from region to region, they had opportunity to meet many in spheres of influence. The ruling spirits met and confronted them upon arrival. These spirits had gained access in that place of influence and power and did not go down without a fight. Apostles and prophets are meant to have the same access to such places because of the level of favor on them and their rank in the spirit. This further demonstrates the kingdom with signs and wonders.

Apostles provide wisdom, clarity, instruction, identity, and understanding to prophets, and without those elements in operation, being implemented, realized and utilized, a prophet will stay stuck in obscurity, unable to advance in their calling and destiny.

Prophets are the word and reveal the word, but apostles build a blueprint and explanation upon the word, so clarity and fullness can come forth.

Prophets are spokesman's for God who stand in his counsel and authority, and who represent his character and righteousness in the earth. They speak to the moral and religious abuses, which so often plagues society and the church of Jesus Christ and legislate the laws of God in the earth.

Apostles are sent ones, (as Jesus was sent by his father, Jesus also sends apostles). They are messengers of God who operate first in rank according to the necessity of leadership in the earthly realm and for the overcoming in the heavenly realms against principalities, powers, rulers of darkness and so on (**Ephesians 6**). They are entrusted with the planting and organization of the church and the dissemination of the gospel to the world. The apostle operates in many realms of authority so as to deliver, heal, bring salvation, show forth God's power in miracles, signs and wonders.

As apostles help prophets come into their office and unique blueprint, a prophet will begin to flourish alongside the apostle in advancing and establishing the government of God in the earth. Part of the co-governing works as they each in their unique calling, blueprint and authority, work closely together to see the overthrowing of hell's agenda's in regions and territories.

One of the greatest stories that speaks to the necessity of this unique covenant relationship, is found in the book of John. Here Jesus is walking on the seashore, after being raised from the dead. He was looking to connect with the disciples once again before he left the earth.

> **John 21:4-7** *"Early in the morning, Jesus stood on the shore, but the disciples did not realize that it was Jesus. He called out to them, "Friends, haven't you any fish?" "No," they answered. He said, "Throw your net on the right side of the boat and you will find some." When they did, they were unable to haul the net in because of the large number of fish. Then the disciple whom Jesus loved said to Peter, "It is the Lord!" As soon as Simon Peter heard him say, "It is the Lord," he wrapped his outer garment around him (for he had taken it off) and jumped into the water.*

We see here the importance of the prophet to the apostle, as John was the one that revealed to Peter that it was Jesus on the shore. Peter did not recognize that it was Jesus, and John although is recognized as an apostle, he also operated as prophet in revealing who Jesus is to the apostles. Consider the following excerpt from the first chapter of the gospel of John:

> **John 1:1-14** *"In the beginning was the Word, and the Word was with God, and the Word was God. He was with God in the beginning. Through him all things were made; without him nothing was made that has been made. In him was life, and that life was the light of all mankind. The light shines in the darkness, and the darkness has not overcome it." There was a man sent from God whose name was John. He came as a witness to testify concerning that light, so that through him all might believe. He himself was not the light; he came only as a witness to the light. The true light that gives light to everyone was coming into the world. He was in the world, and though the world was made through him, the world did not recognize him. He came to that which was his own, but his own did not receive him. Yet to all who did receive him, to those who believed in his name, he gave the right to become children of God— children born not of natural descent, nor of human decision or a husband's will, but born of God. The Word became flesh and made his dwelling among us. We have seen his glory, the glory of the one and only Son, who came from the Father, full of grace and truth."*

Sounds like someone doing a lot of revealing right? John is listed among the founding twelve apostles, but scripture reveals him in the role of prophet and evangelist. It is John the revelator, who told Apostle Peter it was Jesus on the shore calling out to them that day as they sat there hopeless after fishing all night. Without that revelation, Peter may have missed his moment of restoration on the shore that was soon to follow. John would many times operate in the role of prophet even though he was a founding apostle. Apostles many times move in an out of operating in the other five-fold gifts and offices as is needed for the building and establishing of the kingdom, so never put God in a box where an apostle is concerned.

We must remember that apostles are first in rank and order according to scripture.

> **1Corinthians 12:27-30** *"All of you together are Christ's body, and each of you is a part of it. Here are some of the parts God has appointed for the church:*
>
> - *first are apostles,*
> - *second are prophets,*
> - *third are teachers,*

> - *then those who do miracles,*
> - *those who have the gift of healing,*
> - *those who can help others,*
> - *those who have the gift of leadership,*
> - *those who speak in unknown languages.*
>
> *Are we all apostles? Are we all prophets? Are we all teachers? Do we all have the power to do miracles? Do we all have the gift of healing? Do we all have the ability to speak in unknown languages? Do we all have the ability to interpret unknown languages? Of course not!"*

Order is necessary when building or establishing anything, so we must understand the kingdom of God is no different. Apostles are first in rank and order and hold the blueprint for building the kingdom. Prophets are second in rank and order so that what is built is upheld in the spirit through revelation, spirit and truth. As heaven makes adjustments, prophets hear, see and know what those adjustments are, and the apostles know how to carry out and implement those blueprints. God gave the church apostles and prophets to build, protect and mature the body of Christ and to establish his kingdom in the earth around the globe. Without these two grace gifts, the church misses out on the blueprints of God for regions and territories and the ranking of authority needed to see these territories transformed for the glory of God.

> **Ephesians 4:14-16** *"Then we will no longer be immature like children. We won't be tossed and blown about by every wind of new teaching. We will not be influenced when people try to trick us with lies so clever they sound like the truth. Instead, we will speak the truth in love, growing in every way more and more like Christ, who is the head of his body, the church. He makes the whole body fit together perfectly. As each part does its own special work, it helps the other parts grow, so that the whole body is healthy and growing and full of love."*

Prophetic Word -The Restoration of the Gift of the Apostle to the Earth

This is a word from the Lord given to Prophet Dana Wade. On May 1, 2019, I was awakened a little after midnight, to an encounter with the Lord. In the encounter I sensed the heart of Father God for the grace gift and office of the apostle. His love, desire and heart for the apostle was very much impressed upon me as I laid there listening to his voice. I had a sense that hell really hated the office and gift of the apostle, but that Father God really loved them. Depending on the streams of ministries that you follow, or church you attend, you may not hear much about the role of the apostle in the New Testament church of today. However, that is not the New Testament of the Bible.

> **Ephesians 2:19-22** *"Consequently, you are no longer foreigners and strangers, but fellow citizens with God's people and also members of his household, **built on the foundation of the apostles and prophets**, with Christ Jesus himself as the chief cornerstone. In him the whole building is joined together and rises to become a holy temple in the Lord. And in him you too are being built together to become a dwelling in which God lives by his Spirit."*

In this time with the Lord, I really had the strong sense not only of his love but the honor for the apostle. It is being restored in the earth. Minds will change about who they are and what they bring as a gift to the church and earth. I think we many times forget that the culture of heaven is one of love but honor as well.

The culture of heaven is love. — Prophet Dana Wade

Apostles are builders and reformers and are foundation to kingdom work and expansion. They have a grace to plow, build and work and that's why they operate so strongly in the ox and Nehemiah anointing. The ox anointing is a plowing anointing that brings an ease, strength and endurance to work, as in co-laboring with the Lord. It is a finishing anointing to be steadfast and faithful and to endure hardships, heartaches and heavy loads. It empowers you to serve in all types of situations and conditions. It enables you to fight the good fight of faith as a good soldier of Jesus. A Nehemiah anointing is a reviving anointing that causes people to get up out of complacency and work together, each in their perspective callings and gifts to build the kingdom of God.

> **Rev. 4:6-7** *"Also in front of the throne there was what looked like a sea of glass, clear as crystal. In the center, around the throne, were four living creatures, and they were covered with eyes, in front and in back. The first living creature was like a lion, the second was like an ox, the third had a face like a man, the fourth was like a flying eagle."*

The ox is one of the manifestations or faces of Christ mentioned here in this passage of scripture. The gospel of Matthew points to Jesus as the ox face of God, Luke is the human face, and John is the face of the eagle.

A lot of prophetic pictures and art are presented with three of these faces- except for the ox. Why? Because the ox is a picture of servanthood, hard work, and diligence. We don't like the work associated with the ox anointing, but God knows that this is such a necessary component of building, and he entrusted it to the apostle. Is it only for the apostle? No, it is not as it is for all those connected to the apostolic vision. However, apostles have a grace to work, plow and build more than the normal person in God's kingdom, so they operate in it as a lifestyle. Not everyone can carry such a yoke on their shoulders long term, but God gave the apostle a strength and a grace to shoulder such loads. As I was sensing all of this with the Lord, I sensed his desire to honor apostles in the earth. We often speak of Jesus as the Great Shepherd, and indeed he is. I love this depiction of Jesus as one who watches over us, guarding us and protecting us from all forms of harm and injury. But Jesus was also the greatest apostle, and we so need to remember that we need this aspect of him too. Many refer to Jesus as a carpenter, but he was really a stone mason. He is after-all the stone the builders rejected, who became the chief cornerstone. And that is what I want to share with you today. I sense the restoration of this office coming to regions on a greater scale, teaming up with prophets to build and expand the kingdom for such a time as this. I sensed from Father God that a regional anointing was coming upon the office of apostle and prophet to work together along with the office of the evangelist. I sensed it on a global scale. God the Father loved the world so much that he sent us the greatest Apostle, Jesus Christ, and he is once again gathering, appointing, commissioning and sending his apostles, to establish his kingdom in the regions of the earth.

The apostle has the rank and jurisdiction in the spirit to overthrow principalities and territorial spirits that have ruled regions for decades, and for centuries in some cases. The fear of the Lord, signs, wonders and miracles are all manifestations that exist in apostolic work. Multiplication, increase, and a gathering of souls is all a part of this joint labor between the apostle, prophet and evangelist. It's a three-corded strand of God's grace that is not easily broken.

The apostle is the sign that points to the greater miracles and works of Jesus. It is the sign of a New Testament church and the reformation that is taking place as God assembles the picture and face of Jesus again in the Lion (Evangelist), Ox (Apostle) and Eagle (Prophet). It was the Acts of the Apostles where God demonstrated his Spirit, power, and mighty works, and it is happening again. Without the Apostle in operation in the earth we are not seeing the fullness of the kingdom in operation, and that is not acceptable to God. Honor is returning to the apostle.

Homework Explorations
1. Journal your revelations regarding Prophet Dana's journey as she walked with Apostle Taquetta.

2. Journal your insights regarding the revealing of a prophet as he or she journey's with an apostle.
3. Journal how leaders in your life have impacted your life, destiny, and calling.
4. Journal your thoughts regarding the prophetic word God gave concerning the rise of apostles and prophets.

Kingdom Nuggets for The Office of a Prophet

By: Prophet Reenita Keys, Vision Carrier of Kingdom Shifters Ministries, Muncie Indiana

Prophetic Assignments

If you are called to the ministry of the prophet, make sure you know your prophetic assignments and sphere of influence each season (naturally and spiritually). You cannot guide the vision or give direction if you are not aware of the assignments God is releasing to you as a prophet. The Lord will give you seasonal assignments to work on personally, regionally, nationally, or internationally depending on the mandate he is releasing over you. Prophetic assignments may change once the door to that assignment closes or upon completion. There are some assignments that will never change because it is a part of the mandate on your life. This is why it is important to know what you are to work on daily, weekly, monthly, seasonally, yearly, and futuristically.

Prophets are God's visionaries. – Prophet Reenita Keys

Mature prophets are builders for the kingdom of heaven. They are God's marked visionaries who have the capacity to see decades ahead of their time. Since prophets can see and hear futuristically, they must teach themselves how to focus. **Do not allow your office to become your dysfunction** where you are getting ahead of God's timing concerning what he is entrusting to you. Be present with him even as you are futuristic in advancing with him.

Prophets have a lot of heavenly encounters. It is okay to have moments when you are caught up in the clouds of heaven but do not allow that to become your weakness where your experiences are not producing the insights and foresights of God. This is spiritual flightiness as well as a sign of immaturity. Being able to engage heaven but not being able to produce the fruit, sound, word, and judgment of heaven is a sign that you are operating in the gift but not the office of a prophet. Prophets are the eyes and ears within fivefold paradigms. They are the ones who identify the movement of God. The prophetic office shares the intricate strategies of God to point people, ministries, and churches in the right direction. Your heavenly encounters must bring heaven to earth. Be intentional to acquire the min, heart, will, and purpose of God through your heavenly encounters. SHIFT!

> ***Amos 3:7-8*** *Surely the Lord God does nothing, Unless He reveals His secret to His servants the prophets. A lion has roared! Who will not fear? The Lord God has spoken! Who can but prophesy?*

Signs, wonders, and supernatural encounters are not to become prophet's idolatry. Prophetic people tend to make everything around them prophetic. They will attempt to find God in everything. I noticed when repetition is evident, prophets automatically believe God is speaking to them. God will speak to us in many ways but **make sure you are not creating your own words out of coincidence**. When God speaks, he is speaking to us for a reason. When you allow flightiness to guide your assignments as a prophet, you have the potential to misguide and misdirect God's people. It is important to judge every word you receive. This is a reason it is imperative for churches and ministries to have prophetic presbyteries who can judge prophetic words for validity. Prophets are God's messengers who carry the wind of heaven in their mouth. This fivefold office has clearance to know the secret intel of God before he brings those plans forth. Knowing your assignments as a prophet brings clear definition and stamina to build upon every word God desires to establish in the earth.

Prophetic Purity
It is important for prophets to stand in position and strategically align themselves to the places they are called to. In today's society, we see many prophets being released into the nations as a form of validation for their prophetic calling. There is such a fascination with international ministry and a negative stigma placed on prophets who are solely called to a church. It grieves me when the body of Christ place so much importance on national ministry that we create a false hierarchy of platforms. If you are called to a local assembly, city, or ministry, your mantle and assignments are just as important as one launched into international ministry. We have beautified platforms to such a high standard that we have created our own version of Hollywood within the church. The thought of this is scary and makes me want to cry out for the body of Christ. It is okay to have a mandate for the nations, but do not allow a passport stamp to measure your prophetic accuracy and alignment. As a prophet you must continually die to the flesh and continually check the motives of your heart.

> ***Galatians 5:24-26*** *Keep in mind that we who belong to Jesus, the Anointed One, have already experienced crucifixion. For everything connected with our self - life was put to death on the cross and crucified with Messiah. We must live in the Holy Spirit and follow after him. So may we never be arrogant, or look down on another, for each of us is an original. We must forsake all jealousy that diminishes the value of others.*

Prophets must hate sin and love purity. There is a fine line between true prophetic ministry and divination. When you live through the purity of the Lord as a lifestyle, it will shield you from demonic entrapments. The average person who hears the word purity will immediately think about being abstinent from sex. Prophetic people must guard what they watch, hear, speak, engage, and come into agreement with. Purity is more than abstaining from sex. Every believer must guard their heart and be mindful of the company they keep. What you allow within the gates of your heart has the power to become an idol. When sin issues and defilement enter the heart, it has the potential to compromise everything regarding your destiny, calling, and office. The snake that seduces you today can become the dragon you will need to slay later if you do not guard your heart. This includes offense.

> *The snake that seduces you today can become the dragon you will need to slay later . . ..* – Prophet Reenita Keys

Proverbs 4:23 *So above all, guard the affections of your heart, for they affect all that you are. Pay attention to the welfare of your innermost being, for from there flows the wellspring of life.*

The devil understands the dominion and authority that was placed on your life. He will use anything he can to sift your purity and peace. He has knowledge that if he can attack your purity, he can taint the office.

Luke 22:31-32 *"Peter, my dear friend, listen to what I'm about to tell you. Satan has obtained permission to come and sift you all like wheat and test your faith. But I have prayed for you, Peter, that you would stay faithful to me no matter what comes. Remember this: after you have turned back to me and have been restored, make it your life mission to strengthen the faith of your brothers."*

Each season continually pray for the fear of the Lord to increase on your life. The fear of the Lord will fortify you from diverting to an alternate route of destruction that wants to disrobe your sonship and inheritance. Many ministers today do not have the fear of the Lord. As a prophet, the fear of the Lord will quicken you to constantly check the posture of your heart. Prophetic people must submit themselves to a posture of persistent healing and deliverance. This stature will keep your prophetic gates clear from various forms of wickedness that would love to block your communication with God. As a fivefold officer, you are set apart from the world no matter what everyone else is doing. Do not allow the enemy to desensitize you from the wiles of the enemy. You must fervently seek purity as if your life depended upon it. If you are prophesying through your soul issues that is divination. Any door outside of Jesus Christ is not authorized. The fear of the Lord will cause you to follow prophetic protocols to test the validity of each prophetic word you receive.

The Chief Cornerstone

The prophetic is not an avenue to showcase your gift, office, or accuracy. Unfortunately, this happens when prophets allow their gift to fulfill the voids in their life. If you are looking to be America's next top prophet, you are deciding to potentially become one of the biggest witches in the nation. No matter how successful you become, always make sure your knees are taller than your shoulders. Run after sonship with God, the Father. Jesus is the only master chief prophet and the perfect role model for prophetic ministry. He is the only chief cornerstone!

> ***Ephesians 2:19-22*** *Now, therefore, you are no longer strangers and foreigners, but fellow citizens with the saints and members of the household of God, having been built on the foundation of the apostles and prophets, Jesus Christ Himself being the chief cornerstone, in whom the whole building, being fitted together, grows into a holy temple in the Lord, in whom you also are being built together for a dwelling place of God in the Spirit.*

It is important for prophets to resist relying on their emotions to navigate how they choose to stir their prophetic wells to release a word. Prophets hear and see the secrets of God. Prophetic people must continually look for consistent heavenly downloads. Jesus operated from the third heavens when prophesying, teaching, and carrying out various assignments. Jesus spoke the word of the Lord continuously and was the word made flesh. He delivered judgment to the wicked powers that possessed and oppressed regions, nations, and people. Jesus did not prophesy the people happy or water down the authenticity of what he heard. Jesus did not fear breaking the laws of the land in order to bring forth the word of the Lord. There are many people in the bible we can relate to depending on our seasons and what we are processing through. At the end of the day, I encourage every prophet to be more like Jesus. He is ultimately the best role model anyone could ask for. As time continues to change, we live in a world that loves to chase after power and influence. Every believer should chase after sonship more than they seek to prophesy. Sonship will continue to reveal your identity that can only be found in God. Prophesying is a verb and it is something you do. The devil is not after your office, he is after your sonship as he knows it strips your identity. Jesus knew the power of being a son, being the son in identity, destiny, and calling. Decreeing you chase after sonship. SHIFT!

Prophetic Scrolls

Prophetic consumption is the eating and digestion of prophetic words that are to be broken up and consumed like scrolls of honey. We can consume the word of the Lord when prophets and prophetic voices strike the atmosphere with the words of the Lord that are gushed out from the Holy Spirit. Prophets should view the words of God as nourishment, delight, and fulfillment, and digest them as manna no mature how challenging they maybe to consume. For all the words of God, whether for rebuke, correction, warning, blessing, edification, are the feast of heaven that makes the body whole and healthy. As prophets continue to value and embody God's words in this fashion, they are able to translate that as they release the word to others, where they not only receive the word but an impartation of it being the sacred feast of God in their lives.

> ***Ezekiel 3:1-3*** *The voice said to me, "Son of man, eat what I am giving you—eat this scroll! Then go and give its message to the people of Israel." So I opened my mouth, and he fed me the scroll. "Fill your stomach with this," he said. And when I ate it, it tasted as sweet as honey in my mouth.*

The Prophetic Office Versus the Gift
Prophecy is not an office; it is a gift. Often, we mistake the gift of prophecy for the office. Anyone can have the gift of prophecy but that does not make them a prophet. Prophecy is not exclusive to the prophet or the fivefold. The Holy Spirit gave many gifts and God wants everyone to prophesy.

> ***Romans 12:6*** *In his grace, God has given us different gifts for doing certain things well. So if God has given you the ability to prophesy, speak out with as much faith as God has given you.*

When you have the gift of prophecy, you can stir up the gift, but you do not have the same authority or jurisdiction one in the office a prophet. Those who flow through the gift of prophecy can prophesy through a grace the Holy Spirit is placing upon them in that time. In the New Testament, the office of a prophet is an identity. Prophet is a noun that describes a class of people who govern a fivefold office. Prophets can govern and judge prophecies that are released. The authority prophets carry in the spirit realm gives them the ability to discern quickly, break demonic powers and strongholds. The office of a prophet is an adjective. It qualifies the candidate and brings forth a governmental jurisdiction and authority.

The anointing is like fresh oil poured upon the prophet to have the grace to birth and plow the work of God. Prophets must make sure they are not prophesying from their own knowledge, instinct, intuition, or predetermination, and must be aware to stop prophesying when the anointing lifts. This is how many prophets quickly become diviners. They enter into a place of releasing words from a soulish dimension that did not come from God.

The Prophetic Seat
If you sit in the office of a prophet, you also have the gift of prophecy. When you are arising as a prophet, you will need to make sure you are not operating out of the grace of your gift. Prophets have such a strong grace to prophecy they may not realize they have not remained seated in their prophetic seat. Personally, prophesying can come easy for me since I have the faith that I can open my mouth and God will fill it.

> **Psalm 81:10** *For it was I, the Lord your God, who rescued you from the land of Egypt. Open your mouth wide, and I will fill it with good things.*

I did not realize that I was leaning and pulling on the grace of the prophetic gift that I was not remaining seated in the office. When I would prophecy, the Lord began to reveal the difference between the two as I prophesied. I noticed when I would initially share words, I would hear and see to a certain extent. Upon SHIFTING into the office of a prophet, it was an evident dimension of power that would rest upon me when prophesying. I would see the person's past, present, and future depending on what God wanted to speak to them. I could feel my governmental prophetic mantle and office resting upon my shoulders. The distinction between the gift and the office was apparent. Prophets may not realize they are only operating through a measure since they have not taken a seat in their office. When you take a seat in the prophetic office it opens an unlimited access of God's power and authority.

Crushing Within Our Prophetic Mantles and Capacities
A lot of people speak about the call and fruit of the prophetic, but people rarely talk about the crushing that takes place in and out of season. The crushing within your heart, soul, mind, character, nature, and the very dimensions that make up who you are. The crushing that causes your will to break. The crushing that causes your posture to remain humble. The crushing that causes you to depend solely on the Lord. The crushing that causes a prophet to be a well of consistent deliverance in a time of bold defilement as the world evolves into blatant sin. The crushing that takes place in order to remain pure, holy, whole, and set apart. The crushing that causes a separation from those seeking his heart and those seeking a platform. The crushing that separates true prophetic voices from those functioning in witchcraft and the "next big name." The crushing that separates servants from those who want to be served. The crushing that causes every place within your capacity to be dethroned for God to be exalted! A prophet has to love the crushing seasons although it is not fun. It brings great promotions as you submit to the process.

Jesus understood the crushing process before he went to the cross. In some crushing seasons, you may feel as if something is dying or you are dying. This phase may feel as if something is dying within your heart. It may feel overwhelming at times and may even cause you to question your process. It was so intense that even Jesus asked for God to delivery him from his suffering.

> ***Matthew 26:38-39*** *And he said to them, "My heart is overwhelmed and crushed with grief. It feels as though I'm dying. Stay here and keep watch with me." Then he walked a short distance away, and overcome with grief, he threw himself face down on the ground and prayed, "My Father, if there is any way you can deliver me from this suffering, please take it from me. Yet what I want is not important, for I only desire to fulfill your plan for me." Then an angel from heaven appeared to strengthen him.*

In this passage of scripture, an angel had to come strengthen Jesus himself in the crushing so he could carry out the assignment that was on his life to fulfill. This is important for prophets to be aware of when they are going through crushing seasons. You will need to pray for God to give you the strength to keep moving forward. The crushing will happen throughout your walk with God before significant SHIFTS. It kills everything that cannot go with you in the next season of your life. You may feel grieved in your spirit because the old things are dying.

> ***Isaiah 43:18-19*** *"Do not remember the former things, Nor consider the things of old. Behold, I will do a new thing, Now it shall spring forth; Shall you not know it? I will even make a road in the wilderness And rivers in the desert.*

There is a breaking that happens when you are being processed into your call. Your response to the crushing will reveal what you are truly ready for. Many do not make it through these processes! This is why many are called, and a few are chosen. Many fivefold candidates abort the process rather than stay the course with God.

> ***Matthew 22:14-15*** *For everyone is invited to enter in, but few respond in excellence.*

Being SHIFTED into your office is not taking a class and getting your name stamped on a paper. It is a process! There are certain things you will need clearances for to handle the deeper things of God. He will not SHIFT you into something you are not ready for.

<u>Characteristics of A Prophet</u>
The prophetic should point people to God. Prophets minister through the heart of God to bring counsel to his people. Prophets will be required to work on their character.

The fruit of your character determines the quality of your prophesy. If the delivery of the word does not match the tone or heart of God, the message becomes corrupted. Often, prophets become bitter, mean-spirited, haughty, or prideful because of challenges experiences from the past. Do not become a prophet who blames everything on their "call" or "anointing." I have met many prophets who did not have the character of God in certain areas of their life. They were quick to validate their actions and responses on being a prophet that judges. Although prophets judge, do not allow personal judgements to override the heart of God within you.

You cannot take it personal if you do not get the response you thought you would receive delivering a prophetic word. Everyone is not your enemy. The devil wants you to think you are always rejected, pushed to the side, overlooked, or silenced. These are places of insecurity and warfare against your identity that you will need to deal with. This can also be a form of subtle pride you will be blinded by since you are blaming everyone else for your issues. If you notice a pattern where people tend to "treat" you a certain way check your pride. Do not be so quick to make your personal biases and offense a prophetic word where you are allowing the devil to validate your soul issues. If you are offended by someone God is not going to give you a word concerning them in that time. God will deal with you before he gives you a word about the other person. He is not a God that will give you a word to dig a deeper hole for your offense.

> ***Matthew 18:21-22*** *Later Peter approached Jesus and said, "How many times do I have to forgive my fellow believer who keeps offending me? Seven times?" Jesus answered, "Not seven times, Peter, but seventy times seven times!*

Prophets will need to operate through unlimited forgiveness. Jesus told Peter he needed to forgive fellow believers that offended him seventy times seven times. If you do the calculations, we are supposed to forgive 490 times daily. Pride is a virus that pierces into the soul of a prophet.
There is a clear distinction between pure confidence versus pride. I have seen a number of prophets become arrogant because of the level of accuracy or anointing they SHIFTED into. Prophets must cast themselves down daily! The spirit of pride is a sneaky culprit that will suffocate and squeeze the purity you carry. Do not allow bad character to corrupt your access to greater doors and opportunities.

Prophets operate through unlimited forgiveness. -Prophet Reenita Keys

> ***1 Corinthians 15:33-34*** *So stop fooling yourselves! Evil companions will corrupt good morals and character. Come back to your right senses and awaken to what*

is right. Repent from your sinful ways. For some have no knowledge of God's wonderful love. You should be ashamed that you make me write this way to you!

A few characteristics of a prophet include the following:

Prophets warn. Prophets will see attacks before the enemy has a chance to violate the people of God. Prophets will have the discernment, knowledge, and tools needed to stand in the watchtower. Prophets will see what others may not see. They partner with the wisdom of God to know the difference between being paranoid of an attack and a true warning. The devil would love to make prophets paranoid about false attacks to cause anxiety, fear, unnecessary warfare, and division. It is important for prophets to cleanse with the blood of Jesus from old tactics of war, contentions, and isolation. These attacks come to pull prophets from the watchtower. When prophets are distracted it leaves ministries, regions, and churches vulnerable for attacks.

> ***Habakkuk 2:1*** *I will climb up to my watchtower and stand at my guardpost. There I will wait to see what the Lord says and how he will answer my complaint.*

Prophets can see through the masks, smoking mirrors, and deception. They can warn leadership about those sent to infiltrate the vision. There are times the enemy will send people to unknowingly disrupt the unity, momentum, and stamina of what they are building in that region. Prophets can quickly identify false prophets who are unassuming wolves who come as a sheep. Mature prophets know how to handle this information without being mean to the people. Despite the spirit someone may be operating in, a prophet must stay within the heart and character of God when warning and expose the ungodly and the false.

> ***Matthew 7:15*** *Constantly be on your guard against phony prophets. They come disguised as lambs, appearing to be genuine, but on the inside they are like wild, ravenous wolves!*

The Awakening of The Watchmen in the Watchtower Prophetic Word
By: Prophet Reenita Keys March 14, 2014

There is a watchtower that oversees the city and it is time for the word of The Lord to go forth like never before. As the sword of The Lord is established into the lighthouse, there will be an explosive eruption of the light of God that will go forth, and his glory will go in every direction from this tower for all to see. A sound will alarm. My people will search the land and will know this sound. Their spirit shall arise and they shall run towards their father's voice like never before. The army of The Lord will strategically activate around the world, but it will start in the sprit realm. I hear The Lord saying, awakening the people of the land so they will see the gift I have before them. My champions will arise in the north. They will arise in the east. They will arise in the west. And they shall arise in the south. The clock is ticking, and the sound of awakening has come to awaken thee from your sleep. STAND UP watchmen of the tower and let my light be established in the kingdom of darkness that I named "earth". Let the utterance come from my womb as I birth thee into the catapult of deviation. Let the roar of turmoil come from the mouth of the prophetic and push back every spirit of witchcraft, high place, principality, king, monster, warlock, illusion, blood seed, locust, evil and plan of the dead.

Prophets war against hell

It is important to know that you war against the principalities and powers. Prophets have an innate mandate to either be black or white on paper. They are either all in or all out when it comes to any matter. Prophets are God's governors who learn how to rise above the attacks sent from hell. Prophets carry the word of the Lord in their mouth to break down demonic structures and evict the wicked powers that terrorize God's people. Prophets tend to learn hands on since their life testifies against hell.

Ephesians 6:12 Your hand-to-hand combat is not with human beings, but with the highest principalities and authorities operating in rebellion under the heavenly realms. For they are a powerful class of demon-gods and evil spirits that hold this dark world in bondage.

Prophets are wired to war against the pit of hell. Each season brings a different war strategy to draw the people out of bandage. Each prophetic blueprint downloaded within a prophet's mandate for that season allows God to teach their hands to war and their fingers to fight against the gates of hell.

Matthew 16:17-19 I give you the name Peter, a stone. And this truth of who I am will be the bedrock foundation on which I will build my church—my legislative assembly, and the power of death will not be able to overpower it! I will give you the keys of heaven's kingdom realm to forbid on earth that which is forbidden in heaven, and to release on earth that which is released in heaven.

Prophets SHIFTS atmospheres
Prophets carry the *Ruach* wind of God that will SHIFT atmospheres. This is a spiritual expression that represents the spirit of God manifesting like a blast of wind. Every prophet should have the confidence that they carry the atmosphere of heaven within them. When a prophet opens their mouth the presence of God explodes around them because they are an ambassador sent from heaven. Prophets need to stay ready and prepared to be used in any given moment to SHIFT the atmosphere to another level within services, meetings, and events no matter the size of the gathering.

Prophets are intercessors
Prophetic people have a strong burden for prayer and intercession. They are called to a life of prayer. This is also a secret place for prophets to commune with God. Prophetic intercession allows prophets to stand in the gap and repair anything they are assigned to pray for. Ezekiel is the perfect example of a prophet who lived a life of intercession.

Ezekiel 22:30 *I looked for someone who might rebuild the wall of righteousness that guards the land. I searched for someone to stand in the gap in the wall so I wouldn't have to destroy the land, but I found no one.*

Ezekiel 4:4-8: *Now lie on your left side and place the sins of Israel on yourself. You are to bear their sins for the number of days you lie there on your side. I am requiring you to bear Israel's sins for 390 days—one day for each year of their sin. After that, turn over and lie on your right side for 40 days—one day for each year of Judah's sin. "Meanwhile, keep staring at the siege of Jerusalem. Lie there with your arm bared and prophesy her destruction. I will tie you up with ropes so you won't be able to turn from side to side until the days of your siege have been completed.*

Ezekiel was a prophet who literally conducted intercession through the prophetic acts and instructions he received from God. Prophets must be willing to give up their lives and make the sacrifices needed to bring that word forth. Ezekiel was devoted and souled out to the call that was on his life.

Prophets create wealth
God wants us wealthy. He does not want his people struggling in poverty living a life of survival. Prophets have a peculiar imagination that produces witty ideas and

creativity. A prophet must write the ideas down, receive strategy, put things into action, and follow through. Prophetic people have the power to prophesy their success. The people of God must contend for their prosperity and wealth. Many in the body of Christ are breaking the back of the spirit of poverty off of their life and family.

Proverbs 8:18 *Unending wealth and glory come to those who discover where I dwell. The riches of righteousness and a long, satisfying life will be given to them.*

Prophets save people from sin

Prophets do not like sin, and they hate everything about it. Prophets are hardwired to see the demons that are blatant, hidden, and connected to sin issues. Demons hate prophets because they can see them so clearly and cast them out. It is a mutual hate, but prophets must be released by God to deal with those sin issues. When people are sinning, prophets tend to naturally feel irritable, stirred, or grieved even if they are not aware of the details. Prophets will need to be okay that they cannot save everybody. There are times you will have to give people space and room to grow or else you will easily become their crutch or idol. Prophets are counselors at heart who always have a plan or strategy to execute break the powers of hell. Many prophets have to be okay that some people will have to learn the hard way and it is that person's choice if they want to come out of sin.

Prophets have a deliverance mandate

Prophecy plays a major role within healing and deliverance ministry. When prophets prophesy to a person you are bringing them into the enlightenment and vision of the Lord. Prophecy will cast down strongholds, while filling a person with the presence and perseverance of the Lord. When someone is going through healing or deliverance they are being gutted out. Prophecy fills those places back up with the knowledge, revelation, blueprints, strength, and equipment that you need to bring those things to past. The prophetic also brings full restoration upon their soul. It is important to speak up and ask for clarity if you are receiving a word in error or feel confused. Those words are filling those areas and embedding them your sphere of influence. It is okay to ask for more instruction and clarity concerning a prophetic word to truly know what is being imparted into your spirit.

Prophets give authentic feedback

Do not ask a prophet what they think about something if you do not want truthful in-depth feedback. Prophets can record events and situations that need to be worked on. They can pinpoint the SHIFTS, areas of opportunities, and potential that was missed. Prophets are grieved when true breakthrough does not come into fullness in corporate gatherings. They are aware of the targets God wanted to hit and if those assignments were completed. Often times, prophets can be straight to the point without sugarcoating their words. It is important to take a moment to search what you are to share and what you are to keep to yourself. This also gives greater maturity to decipher your opinion versus the thoughts of God.

Prophets are spontaneous
When you allow your prophets to go forth there is no such thing as a duplicate meeting. The prophetic will allow the Holy Spirit to have full access to your worship, intercession, preaching, and teaching. Religious and traditional spirits do not like this about the prophetic because they would rather keep their services on replay. They will sing the same songs, preach the same sermons, and keep everything scripted. Prophets operate outside of time and cause an acceleration to come upon the people. Prophetic people are change agents. Their presence alone houses the voice of God. Since prophets are ministering from heaven to earth, what would have taken two years may supernaturally take place in one meeting. Prophetic officers cause heaven to breakout.

Homework Explorations
1. Identify the assignments on your life that you are to bring forth as a prophet. What are you doing to actively complete those assignments?
2. Who are the prophetic voices in your life that keep you accountable to your assignments?
3. How can you work on your foundation as a prophet to activate a greater level of maturity?
4. Are there any places where you are seeking validation through your prophetic gift?
5. What are some areas you would like the Holy Spirit to purify and refine in your foundation?
6. Do you function through the gift of prophecy or the office of the prophet?
7. If you are a prophet, do you believe you have functioned solely through the gift of prophecy or the office?
8. How do you handle the crushing moments that happen within your call?
9. What are some places within your life that demonstrate subtle or blatant pride? Spend time journaling to allow the Holy Spirit to expose these places.

The Ox Anointing: Apostolic Ability to Plow and Build

The ox anointing is a pioneering anointing that supernaturally enables apostolic leaders and members to produce manifestation beyond natural means. It enables and empowers those with apostolic ability to labor, work, physically plow, and plow in the Spirit without feeling tired or having much sleep. It propels beyond their natural ability and shifts to supernatural ability for accomplishing what God has set on your agenda. Many apostles have this anointing. Many prophets and fivefold ministers are empowered with this anointing in different seasons, especially when they work alongside an apostle or are part of an apostolic work.

> **Psalms 92:10** *But my horn shalt thou exalt like the horn of an unicorn (wild bull or ox); I shall be anointed with fresh oil.*

Horn is the Hebrew word *qeren* and means *"ray of light, power, strength."*

> **English Standard Bible** *But You have exalted my horn like that of the wild ox; I have been anointed with fresh oil.*

There is continual fresh oil inside the well of an ox. The more they pour out, the more they produce light, power, and strength.

> **Psalms 144:14** *That our oxen may be strong to labour; that there be no breaking in, nor going out; that there be no complaining in our streets. Happy is that people, that is in such a case: yea, happy is that people, whose God is the Lord.*

The strength and labor of the ox provides protection, guarding, and covering from any break-in by thieves, thieving spirits, and demonic attacks.

1Corinthians 15:10 Paul labored more abundantly than all the apostles, yet it was by the grace of God that he labored.

> *But by the grace (the unmerited favor and blessing) of God I am what I am, and His grace toward me was not [found to be] for nothing (fruitless and without effect). In fact, I worked harder (labored) than all of them [the apostles], though it was not really I, but the grace (the unmerited favor and blessing) of God which was with me.*

The ox anointing allows us to supernaturally work harder and produce more than those around us. The ox anointing results in possessing the strength to produce more than many others put together. The more a fivefold leader taps into and embodies the ox anointing, the greater its supernatural strength to produce, reproduce, and multiply rests on the leader.

> ***Psalms 14:4*** *Where no oxen are, the crib is clean: but much increase is by the strength of the ox.*

The ox anointing = harvest. The ox produce harvest within a life, family, generation, ministry, business, region. An ox anointing produces souls because what it produces will draw souls to Christ.

> ***The Message Bible*** *No cattle, no crops; a good harvest requires a strong ox for the plow.*

> ***Proverbs 15:17*** *Better is a dinner of herbs where love is, than a stalled ox and hatred therewith.*

Stalled is *abas* in the Hebrew and means to be "*fat or strong*" in the ox anointing.

Even as the ox anointing is strong and fat, a leader must still possess the love and humility of God.

Even as the ox anointing is strong and fat, a leader must still possess the love and humility of God. Note to reader: You cannot let the strength or confidence of the ox make you prideful, puffed up, hardened against others or even judgmental that they cannot keep up or produce like you do. You must love people for where they are and recognize that this is a supernatural rare strength that is upon you to plant, plow, and build in this season.

> ***1Corinthians 9:9*** *For it is written in the law of Moses, Thou shalt not muzzle the mouth of the ox that treadeth out the corn. Doth God take care for oxen?*

> ***1Timothy 5:17-18*** *Let the elders that rule well be counted worthy of double honour, especially they who labour in the word and doctrine. For the scripture saith, Thou shalt not muzzle the ox that treadeth out the corn. And, The labourer is worthy of his reward.*

You should not muzzle your ox anointing and neither should others. A worthy reward, authority, and double honor comes from operating in the ox anointing. To quench it, quenches the blessings you are to receive from it. You may feel as if you are doing the most and you are, but you will receive a worthy reward for your sacrifice and labor.

Synonyms for ox

burly	hefty	stalwart
beast	hunk	stout
hulking	husky	tall
sturdy	powerful	vigorous
hulk	powerhouse	well-built
brawny	robust	

Homework Explorations

1. As you consider the revelation in this chapter, what reasons do you need the ox anointing for you fivefold ministry?
2. Journal seasons in your life where the ox anointing would have been beneficial in finishing an assignment.
3. Journal your thoughts on what it is like to work with people who do not have endurance or perseverance. Journal how you would empower your team to SHIFT into the supernatural strength of the ox anointing.
4. Consider the synonyms for the ox. Journal on at least five of them and ask the Holy Spirit to empower you with the characteristics of an ox.

The Nehemiah Anointing

Nehemiah 6:13 The Message Bible *When Sanballat, Tobiah, Geshem the Arab, and the rest of our enemies heard that I had rebuilt the wall and that there were no more breaks in it—even though I hadn't yet installed the gates— Sanballat and Geshem sent this message: "Come and meet with us at Kephirim in the valley of Ono." I knew they were scheming to hurt me so I sent messengers back with this: "I'm doing a great work; I can't come down. Why should the work come to a standstill just so I can come down to see you?"*

Do NOT come down from where God has placed you!

When you are BUILDING for God, he is the only one who gets to dictate how you BUILD and what you focus on while you BUILD. Some plans he gives you ahead of time and others you learn as you BUILD with him. Nehemiah was sought after four times to come down and focus on something that was not part of the current building vision. A fifth pursuit of Nehemiah came with accusations, and misperceptions that sounded as if they could have merit. Nehemiah knew they were not of the Lord and were sent to instill fear and weakness, so that he and his team would not BUILD through the strength of the Lord. The visionary always carries the character and nature of the BUILDING vision. This is how Nehemiah knew this was a trick of the enemy. He had become the identity of the plan before he even began BUILDING IT! He had become the wall! He had become the protector of the people, the vision, the region of Jerusalem, and the wall itself they were building. He was now a representation of a repairer of the breach, healer of reproach, and of restoration, and he was not about to leave his mountain for mess and messy people.

The enemy would want you to come down and defend yourself against false prophecy and false delusions, and conspiracy, but do not do it. You have all the defense and prophecies you need at this current time and in the current dimension to which you are BUILDING. Anything contrary to what God is speaking is a false vision of infiltration setting you up to be deterred, stifled, delayed, or destroyed. Do not get into prideful petty tiffs that are not your battle. Stay focused and BUILD IT!

This needs to be your decree in every season: "I Am Doing a Great Work; I Cannot Come Down!"
Do not come down for:
- ❖ Demons

- ❖ People
- ❖ Pettiness
- ❖ Confusion
- ❖ Low or ungodly character and nature
- ❖ Jealousy
- ❖ Discord
- ❖ Strife
- ❖ Emotionalism
- ❖ Sin
- ❖ A good plan that is not God's plan

Become the vision and embody it, so that your essence decrees, "I Am Doing a Great Work; I Cannot Come Down!" SHIFT!

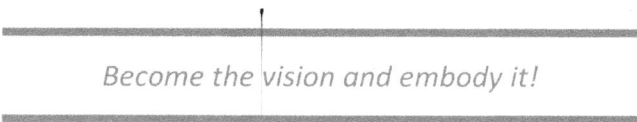

Become the vision and embody it!

Homework Explorations

Study **Nehemiah 1-6**. Write a two page paper on the principles of the Nehemiah anointing, insights on what he implemented to stay on the wall, how he resisted the enemy, and how you should implement these applicable tools in your life and vision to remain focused in BUILDING the vision.

Fivefold Revival Reformation

This chapter is from Dr. Taquetta's book, *Igniting Regional Revival*

Often, we equate revival to a strong, consistent outpouring of God's presence where miracles, signs, and wonders, easily and constantly manifest. This is factual in thought; however, if a ministry is truly mantling revival fire, the revival should eventually impact the following:

- ❖ Land
- ❖ Community
- ❖ Climate
- ❖ Atmosphere
- ❖ Economic Production
- ❖ Political Government
- ❖ Spiritual Enlightenment
- ❖ Family Lifestyle
- ❖ Generational Disposition & Inheritance

The purpose of regional revival is to restore reformation while rebuilding and reestablishing people, lands, atmospheres, climates, and regions in the fullness of salvation. The essential mandate of churches and fivefold ministry is to be an edifice for DAILY reigning and governing God's kingdom and revival fire in the earth, such that salvation reigns in the earth (**See Ephesians 4:11-13).**

True revival is not void of reformation. We know true revival has come to a region when:

- Deliverance, healing, and wellness are evident in people, families, generations, the land, communities, atmospheres, and region.

- The sins and curses of the people and land are broken, producing the production, fruitfulness, fullness, multiplication, subduing, and dominion that God originally designed in **Genesis 1:28**.

- The blessings of **Deuteronomy 28** overtakes the region as people honor the commandments of God with their life.

- A renewal of belief and faith in God is restored into the region.

- The reestablishing of salvation is restored people, families, lands, climate, atmospheres, communities, and regions.

- Whole families serve God as his name and wonders are glorified throughout the generations.

- There is reconciliation and restoration of restored covenant with God where people walk in destiny relationship with him and live through his word, morals, standards, character, and nature.

- People live a lifestyle of prayer, fasting, studying the word, and building themselves up in the identity, destiny, and wellness of God.

- People cry out in repentance and are restored to salvation, just by the presence of God reigning in the region.

- People are added to God's kingdom daily as the fame of regional revival spreads like wildfire, drawing souls within the region and beyond, to be saved and live for Jesus.

- The gifts of the spirit stir and tangibly manifest in the saints and ministries.

- People are consistently equipped, licensed, ordained, and released to walk in their destiny and calling.

- Improvements and amendments of what is wrong, corrupt, unsatisfactory, evil, abusive, out of order, is reordered in the will and purpose of God and his kingdom.

- Change for the betterment of the people, families, lands, climates, atmospheres, and communities is tangible and evident.

- Principalities, powers, and territorial spirits are displaced from the region, and God's Holy principalities - his fivefold ministers - govern and guard the gates of the region.

- High places and hidden covens are torn down, as idols are exposed and dismantled, and witches and warlocks are given an ultimatum to serve God or be judged to damnation.

- The climate and atmospheres of homes, communities and eventually the entire region begins to radiate the goodness, blessing, and glory of God as the region lives under an open heaven where God's covering, protection, government, and kingdom is established and reigns.

- God's government overrides the Worldly system as the political arenas within the community seek Godly counsel and guidance for what laws, standards, and practices should be allowed in the region.

- People seek God and ministries before they consider worldly systems of wellness and success.

- Poverty and lack are SHIFTED out as enough employment, entrepreneurship, opportunities for personal and community advancement, are SHIFTED into the region.

- Rebuilding of the physical face of the communities where walls, businesses, homes, organizations, churches, and the land itself begins to manifest the glory, beauty, wealth, and wellness of God.

- Godly people and ministries become landowners and begin to take back the region for the kingdom of God.

- Godly people and ministries build their own schools and universities to professionally educate and equip the saints in their destiny and calling.

- Godly people and ministries build their own houses, hospitals, wellness centers, banks, stores, malls, counseling centers, gyms, social service agencies, schools, shelters, social ventures; the world pursues the Godly to get their needs and desires met.

Conclusion: We must desire more than a great move of God inside the walls of our church and events. Our mindset and focus must be to takeover the region with the glory and kingdom of God.

Homework Explorations
1. Study the word salvation in the Greek. Journal the attributes of salvation as you search them out in your study and with God.

2. What are your thoughts that revival is daily, and we should always be revived and living renewed in God?
3. What are your thoughts that revival includes reformation and without it, it is not full revival?
4. How can your fivefold ministry awaken revival reformation in your ministry and region?

Shifting with Times and Seasons

Letter to my senior citizen friends,

I am Taquetta's spiritual mother, and I am approaching 70 years old. All of the technology that I own is because Taquetta said, "Mommak, we need to get (fill in the blank) for you." Recently, I bought a new television. I called her and said, "Do you have one of those stick things to put in the back of the tv?" She calmly said, "Mommak, it's a smart tv." That really means the tv is a smarter tv because it is smarter than me! I remember being scared of eating toast from a toaster because the bread jumped up in the air when it was finished. I was used to making toast in the oven. I am still suspicious of microwaves. Backing my SUV up is a challenge for me and never mind the people that have mentioned the back-up camera. It doesn't help me! I heard a preacher many years ago talk about God's signal to the Israelites that it was time to break camp and move on in their journey. "And when the cloud was taken up from the tabernacle, then after that the children of Israel journeyed: and in the place where the cloud abode, there the children of Israel pitched their tents (Exodus 40:17)." The preacher made it simple, "When God says move, you can either go with Him or get left behind." As a young believer (and now), I earnestly prayed, "God, please don't leave me behind. I want to go wherever you are going." If you are in this third journal, then we have a kindred spirit in that we want to God where God is going. I remember hiding under my covers at night to listen to my transistor radio. I wanted to hear the stations from far away. Now, we can listen to satellite radio and listen to people from all over the planet. More than that, we can use that same technology as a way of fulfilling Jesus' instruction that we can go to all the world and teach the gospel. I love David's words about the way generations should learn from one another. "3Great is the LORD and greatly to be praised; His greatness is unsearchable. 4One generation will commend Your works to the next, and they shall proclaim Your mighty acts (Psalm 145:3-4). Blessings, Dr. Kathy Williams

Many Christians, particularly those in the Retirees and Baby Boomer generations, assume the advancement technology and the internet is demonic and was created by the devil. Marketing experts call them *resistors* as they are the last consumer group to accept a new product. In terms of fivefold ministry, it means the group that has not SHIFTED with the times. Many stand by their refusal to SHIFT by singling out the negative impact technology and the internet has had on society, communication, youth, family structure and relationships, laws, moral and values, ideologies and perceptions. Others contend God did not make technology and the internet. Their perception is that it is a conspiracy for the revealing of the antichrist, the mark of the beast, and the tribulation.

While that resistant mindset restricts to a time warp, society SHIFTS to where it is increasingly difficult to navigate everyday life without technology and the internet.

Seventy percent of communication and business ventures have some form of online or technology operations, and despite opposition, this has and continues to become the norm of our society. There was a time that many resisted using cards to swipe for purchases as a sign of the cashless society that would come with the mark of the beast. Though there is some truth to the challenging impact technology and the internet has on society, I want to state that these advancements were not created by the devil. We serve an intelligent, progressive, creative God who is always evolving us and the world we live in. God charged us from the beginning to prosper, have influence in the earth, subdue it, multiply it, and reign over it.

> ***Genesis 1:28*** *And God blessed them, and God said unto them, Be fruitful, and multiply, and replenish the earth, and subdue it: and have dominion over the fish of the sea, and over the fowl of the air, and over every living thing that moveth upon the earth.*

It was never his intent for us to live in a limited scope and not evolve. Adam and Eve were destined to rule. God told them in Genesis 1:26 to have dominion, and that instruction continues to this current time.

When God's people were in Egyptian captivity, God delivered them and promised them prosperity. He promises them power to be prosperous and advance, and he is still doing that today. The conditional promise was based on the people remembering him as Lord and keeping him as the head of their lives. Making sure he was given glory and that they remained reliant on him and not the wealth, and what they created or built. The wealth and inventions were not ungodly but serving them as idol gods was ungodly. It is trusting in riches and not the actual riches that can contaminate someone's spiritual walk.

> ***Deuteronomy 8:19-20*** *But thou shalt remember the LORD thy God: for it is he that giveth thee power to get wealth, that he may establish his covenant which he sware unto thy fathers, as it is this day. And it shall be, if thou do at all forget the Lord thy God, and walk after other gods, and serve them, and worship them, I testify against you this day that ye shall surely perish. As the nations which the Lord destroyeth before your face, so shall ye perish; because ye would not be obedient unto the voice of the Lord your God.*

<u>Powered</u> in Hebrew is *ḥaiyl* and means:
1. a force, whether of men, means or other resources
2. an army, wealth, virtue, valor, strength, able, activity
3. army, band of men (soldiers), company, (great) forces, goods, host, might, power, riches, strength, strong, substance, train,

4. valiant(-ly), valour, virtuous(-ly), war, worthy(-ily)

God was not only giving the Israelites power to get wealth but gave them contentment of knowing that they did not have to return to reliance on Egypt who had enslaved them. God also said he was giving them a team mentality so that they would work together to produce wealthy and economic advancement in their sphere. We learn this through the definition of power which reveals the production of "valiant company of trained soldiers, who would be equipped with his power to produce wealth. This was a fivefold ministry concept being made manifested in the earth even in the early biblical eras.

> ***Proverbs 12:8*** *says, I wisdom dwell with prudence, and find out knowledge of witty inventions.*

God's wisdom is speaking to us in this scripture and is letting us know that within it resides the truth, revelation, and strategy to produce witty inventions. One challenging fact among believers is the truth that secular inventors are more apt to pursue witty ideas without realizing or acknowledging that God is their source of inspiration. Many from that group are more likely to be risktakers and trailblazers to create new works than believers and those of the older generation. That circles us back to the church needing to be introspective and ask, "Why?" It is an uncomfortable but necessary examination.

Consider your experience and review the following statements. How many can you identify as being part of the "stifling" dynamic?

- Being stifled on the pews or within the four walls of the church.
- Staying in the safety of our comfort zones.
- Having a narrow mentality about what is of God, what it means to be God's child, what it means to live for God.
- Rejecting and lacking godly cultivation regarding money, prosperity, and destiny advancement resulting in believers with missed opportunities for wealth, inventions, and to have dominion in the earth.

We have done ourselves a disservice by not seeking wisdom and knowledge on how to have full dominion in the earth. We have failed to rule adequately, while those of the world have taken these visionary opportunities and witty wisdom to heart, implemented them, advanced the times, society, and the earth at large. Now we, the believers, are subject to the kingdom they have built. We are now having to infiltrate these kingdoms and reclaim these inventions, realms of influence, its wealth and impact in the earth for God and his kingdom. Please hear that a major distinction between kingdom mindset and secular mindset is simply that the latter lacks any mechanism to glorify God. This writing is not suggesting that they are "bad" people or that they are all going to hell for not putting some sort of "Praise God" label on their efforts. This writing is not a judgment against the world or secular inventors. It is a prodding of believers to simply ask, "Have you taken your rightful place in our economy and society?"

It is important for those of the older generation and believers in general to recognize that we do not have to SHIFT into the demonic trends, but we do have to SHIFT with the times. We do not have to SHIFT under the demonic demise, morals, and laws of the world, but we do need to SHIFT into being a light in ALL dark places. We do not have to serve wealth and prosperity, but we do need it to advance the kingdom of God. We can be wealthy and prosperous and still live a saved, integral, God-fearing life. If we continue to not seek wisdom and knowledge for witty ideas and SHIFT with the times and seasons, the ungodly and the world and demonic systems will pick up our inheritance in the spirit realm, run with the visions, and reign in dominion in ruling and advancing the earth.

> *Ecclesiastes 9:11* I saw something else under the sun: The race is not to the swift, nor the battle to the strong; neither is the bread to the wise, nor the wealth to the intelligent, nor the favor to the skillful; rather, time and chance happen to all.

This scripture reveals that God is not looking just to believers, he is looking for willing vessels. If he waited on just using believers, we would still be stuck in the horse and buggy era. God is looking for those who are risk takers, who are in momentum with him at the right time and the right circumstances. I am sure he desires it to be his people; however, God is always intentional about getting his work must be done, so he will use a donkey if he must.

We must get off the pews, get out of our old rocking chairs, throw away our black and white TV sets and dial up phones, SHIFT out of our old and erred religious mindsets regarding prosperity, wealth, and ruling in the earth, and SHIFT into the times and chances of God. The world is not waiting on us to catch up. It is leaving us behind, and we are being demanded by laws and happenstance to succumb to its ways, while rebelling through the little tradition we fathom to hold. Because this is our posture, we are failing to rule, failing to reach souls, failing to live in destiny momentum with God, and failing to effectively advance his kingdom. Especially if we have been given a fivefold kingdom vision, we must understand that the vision alone is designed for us to rule, reign, and prosper.

***3John 1:2** Beloved, I wish above all things that thou mayest prosper and be in health, even as thy soul prospereth.*

Prosper is *euodoo* in Greek and means:
1. to help on the road, i.e. (passively) succeed in reaching
2. figuratively, to succeed in business affairs have a prosperous journey
3. to grant a prosperous and expeditious journey
4. to lead by a direct and easy way, to grant a successful issue
5. to cause to prosper, to prosper, be successful

Salvation is about living God's fullness in every area of our lives.

- In health and wellness
- In heart, mind, and soul
- In identity, destiny, and calling
- In family and covenant relationships
- In social relations
- In ministry and destiny visions
- In financial endeavors
- In business and economic interactions
- In safety and protection

We must claim our kingly inheritance to rule in every sphere of salvation. It is our right as believers and sons of God.
Please note that the internet and communication lines are real realms and spheres.

SHIFT! SHIFT RIGHT NOW!

They are atmospheric airways that allow interaction and engagement. As supernatural beings, spirit living in a body, you do not need to be afraid or resistant to these realms. You were meant to reign in every realm that exists. That is why when he told Adam and Eve to have dominion, he mentioned the land, air, and sea. We are to reign in all spheres over all things. Jesus reestablished this truth for us by allowing us to sit in heavenly places with him as he raised from the dead and was restored to the right side of heaven's throne (***Ephesians 2:6***). As these realms have gained momentum, it is important to understand that some of your remnant are in these realms, your destiny and calling is tied to these realms, some of your training is connected to these realms, some of your prosperity and divine connections are associated with these realms, and some of the way you are to build and advance your vision is aligned with these realms. You have authority and jurisdiction in these realms whether you utilize it or not. And we all know that the devil will take up, claim and devour all unclaimed territory.

As you SHIFT into fivefold ministry, SHIFT into these realms where you have influence and can receive all God has for you regarding them as pertinent. Take risks and pursue the witty ideas God gives you. Fivefold ministry is supposed to evolve, progress, and SHIFT the earth. We are not activating fivefold in the exact same way that Paul instructed the Ephesians. We are not wearing sandals or walking deserts. It is not possible to do fivefold ministry and reject the advancement of technology, the internet, and other realms of influence that keeps the world progressing. Especially in this day where people are more and more resistant to being connected to a particular church body, it is essential to utilize every possible tool for reaching souls.

It might seem that this chapter is picking on the older believers; however, that is not the intention. The reason the older generations are highlighted is the transition from a traditional leadership model to a fivefold ministry often engages those who have served in ministry for many decades. It is the seasoned, mature leaders who God is now offering an opportunity to expand into new territory called fivefold ministry. There may be some of you who are reading who know that your denomination is not supportive of the fivefold paradigm. There is no question that it is scary to be called back into pioneering mode! The fivefold manuals are not just a map but a message that you are not doing this alone.

If any of the list below is something you need to do, then have a good laugh and say, "Lord, I am going to do it!" If you have to get a millennial or GenerationY to show you how, then ask for their help!

I CHARGE YOU TO:

- Get a smart phone and learn how to use it!
- Get a computer and learn how to use it!
- Learn how to download and use apps and start engaging in realms and spheres that are rightfully yours.
- Get a Facebook, Twitter, and Instagram page! Pursue your remnant and divine connections all over the world!
- Join some groups and find your tribe and likeminded individuals to SHIFT with.
- Become a web searcher for knowledge and answers while refuting the knowledge and falsehoods that are not of God!
- Build a website, an app, a social media page for your ministry, business, and organization!

- Attend and then facilitate live videos, webinars, groups that help spread the gospel, and train, equip and empower people!
- Come out of the old into the present and on to the new!
- Fearlessly SHIFT into the fullness of all God have for you!

Let's do that list one more time and this time, let's look at it as a checklist. Put a check beside the things you already doing that involve technology. Have you seen the movie *Bucket List*? Let this be your fivefold, kingdom, glory shifting, bucket list!

	Get a smart phone
	Get a computer
	Download apps (software apps)
	Facebook
	Twitter
	Instagram
	Linkedin
	Join a ministry network
	Learn how to "google"
	Learn how to hashtag
	Build a website, app, or social media page
	Attend live videos, webinars
	PRODUCE a live video or webinar
	Get an iPad or other brand of tablet so that you are mobile!

Seasoned leaders, you have experiences that other generations need. Don't become guilty of aborting spiritual legacy! Remember that we never confess, "I can't." We only say, "I haven't learned yet."

> ***1Samuel 2:7-10*** *The Lord maketh poor, and maketh rich: he bringeth low, and lifteth up. He raiseth up the poor out of the dust, and lifteth up the beggar from the dunghill, to set them among princes,*
> *and to make them inherit the throne of glory: for the pillars of the earth are the Lord's, and he hath set the world upon them. He will keep the feet of his saints, and the wicked shall be silent in darkness; for by strength shall no man prevail. The adversaries of the Lord shall be broken to pieces; out of heaven shall he thunder upon them: the Lord shall judge the ends of the earth; and he shall give strength unto his king, and exalt the horn of his anointed.*

Homework Explorations

1. Journal your thoughts regarding this chapter.
2. Read **Proverbs 31.** Journal regarding her power to get wealth and advance the earth. Journal hope you would impact society if you had her wealth and abilities.
3. What are some areas you need to grow as it relates to using technology and the internet to connect with other believers and advance the gospel?
4. How can technology and the internet be utilized in your ministry vision.
5. Study **1Samuel 2:7-10**. Journal the revelation you receive from the scripture as it relates to this chapter.

Bustin' Out of the Four Walls

This chapter and the next two chapters may seem to border on harsh directives, but here is a word of encouragement to you. You are nearing the end of a 3-volume series which means you are dedicated to the change God is orchestrating in your life. From this point forward, read this as if you are an athlete that was just snatched up by your jersey and told by the coach, "Get in the game!" You are no longer on the bench! You have waited for this moment. God is grabbing you by the jersey and telling you, "Get in the game!"

It is easy to become complacent by doing ministry within the four walls of the church and within the church system. We build our own world and become busy ministering to one another. The result is that we are only impacting those who attend services, events and programs. Succumbing to routine, missing vision for community development and revival reformation, and lacking a burden for evangelizing souls are just a few reasons people do not minister outside the four walls of the church. Not wanting the unsaved to mess up the perfect religious church culture that has been built is also a reason people resist regional fivefold ministry. This is religious prejudice. Using another phrase, the outcome is becoming a religious snob. The members have forgotten that they were once sinners, have become smug in their religious activities, positions, and doctrines, hardened and judgmental in their heart against the lost, and have forgotten the true reason for salvation, the gospel, and the church.

"Respect of persons" mentality becomes the model of evangelizing and growing the church. This is done by ministering only to a select few that are deemed appropriate as the members go about their week, and then inviting them to church. Such lucky patrons are usually coworkers, family members, classmates, or people the members usually muster enough courage to evangelize during happenstance encounters or during a Holy Ghost quickening or compassionate moment. Reading the next few sentences is going to be like ripping a Band-Aid off a wound. Hang on past the initial sting, and you will see the value in getting some air to the wound. Though not always the case, I want to expose the haughty churchgoer demon by saying that many of these people are invited as testimony props of how God used them. Furthermore, some people only invite those they know will fit into their church culture or make them look good, while leaving the crack addict, the homeless, and the prostitute on the street. The "quickening" that Jesus sends to nudge a believer to reach out can quickly pass. We must be sensitive to the moment of the assignment. Much of the denial of reaching for others is because the ministry lacks programs and finances to help such populations of people or do not have connections with social service agencies within the community where these people can be immediately assisted. The Bible warns us that a respect of persons mentality is not of God. God did not assign us to do it all but without a community network, we wind up spiritually impotent and incapable of doing anything. That is NOT the will of God.

> **Romans 2:10-12 The Amplified Bible** *But glory and honor and [heart] peace shall be awarded to everyone who [habitually] does good, the Jew first and also the Greek (Gentile).For God shows no partiality [undue favor or unfairness; with Him one man is not different from another]. All who have sinned without the Law will also perish without [regard to] the Law, and all who have sinned under the Law will be judged and condemned by the Law.*

The average believer does not have a heart, mind, or training to evangelize on a daily basis. Having a church body who frequently SHIFTS outside of the ministry to reach the lost and broken is becoming more and more a rarity. There is minimal consistent cultivation of how to utilize the spiritual gift of witnessing to others. When most believers come into a ministry mindset, their focus is on positions within the church. If you suggest ministry outside of the ministry, the religious mindset that has been cultivated in the body of Christ is that this is,

- ❖ Less than and not as glorifying as platform ministry;
- ❖ You just think I want your church or position;
- ❖ They do not want me to be used.

This mentality has become such a stronghold that you literally will have to bust out the four walls of the church to be free from it. The main vision carrier will want to SHIFT slowly to give the members a chance to grasp the change, but I have found that this pacifying posture causes undue warfare as the members emotions as religious complacency controls the tempo, process, and progress of the vision, rather than God and the vision carrier. This also prolongs and stifles the vision. When you BUSTIN' out, you have to engage in a "suddenly" anointing.

Jesus did not give the disciples time to think about their SHIFT!

> **Matthew 4:18-22** *And Jesus, walking by the sea of Galilee, saw two brethren, Simon called Peter, and Andrew his brother, casting a net into the sea: for they were fishers. And he saith unto them, Follow me, and I will make you fishers of men. And they straightway left their nets, and followed him. And going on from thence, he saw other two brethren, James the son of Zebedee, and John his brother, in a ship with Zebedee their father, mending their nets; and he called them. And they immediately left the ship and their father, and followed him.*

***Matthew 19:27-30** Then answered Peter and said unto him, Behold, we have forsaken all, and followed thee; what shall we have therefore? And Jesus said unto them, Verily I say unto you, That ye which have followed me, in the regeneration when the Son of man shall sit in the throne of his glory, ye also shall sit upon twelve thrones, judging the twelve tribes of Israel. And every one that hath forsaken houses, or brethren, or sisters, or father, or mother, or wife, or children, or lands, for my name's sake, shall receive an hundredfold, and shall inherit everlasting life. But many that are first shall be last; and the last shall be first.*

***Luke 9:57-62** And it came to pass, that, as they went in the way, a certain man said unto him, Lord, I will follow thee whithersoever thou goest. And Jesus said unto him, Foxes have holes, and birds of the air have nests; but the Son of man hath not where to lay his head. And he said unto another, Follow me. But he said, Lord, suffer me first to go and bury my father. -- Jesus said unto him, Let the dead bury their dead: but go thou and preach the kingdom of God. And another also said, Lord, I will follow thee; but let me first go bid them farewell, which are at home at my house. And Jesus said unto him, No man, having put his hand to the plough, and looking back, is fit for the kingdom of God.*

***Luke 14:25-35** Now great multitudes went with Him. And He turned and said to them, "If anyone comes to Me and does not hate his father and mother, wife and children, brothers and sisters, yes, and his own life also, he cannot be My disciple. And whoever does not bear his cross and come after Me cannot be My disciple. For which of you, intending to build a tower, does not sit down first and count the cost, whether he has enough to finish it— lest, after he has laid the foundation, and is not able to finish, all who see it begin to mock him, saying, 'This man began to build and was not able to finish'? Or what king, going to make war against another king, does not sit down first and consider whether he is able with ten thousand to meet him who comes against him with twenty thousand? Or else, while the other is still a great way off, he sends a delegation and asks conditions of peace. So likewise, whoever of you does not forsake all that he has cannot be My disciple.*

The disciples had to lay their nets down and immediately follow Jesus. Initially, they did not have time to process or think about the SHIFT. Their processing came after they agreed with Jesus and SHIFTED with him. They could not say goodbye to family, explain their SHIFT, or bury the dead. This represents letting go of anything that is not connected to life and where God is taking you in the fivefold vision, especially if it is dead. Jesus will show you in the new SHIFT what can be part of this new place as you SHIFT with him. But you yourself do not get to determine what goes and what does not go. He determines that! You just have to let go and bury everything and allow him to resurrect it as he evolves you in this new destiny

SHIFT! SHIFT RIGHT NOW! SHIFT!

As God resurrects what he desires to be in your new SHIFT, he will also teach you how to raise the dead. Truly you were a graveyard digger in your old life even if you were not adding to people's dysfunction. Walking in a false or limited identity was only giving yourself and people a measure of the impact you are to have in the earth, and minimal opportunity to journey in the fullness of salvation that came with Jesus resurrecting from the cross. Indeed, you are not reaching your full remnant, so they are not operating in their fullness because they lack your fullness. In this new SHIFT, you SHIFT to raising the dead – your dead remnant, dead people, dead vision - as your identity unveils in fullness and the complete destiny and calling of who you are is released in the earth.

Shift to raising the dead – your dead remnant (generations), dead people, dead vision. Be released in the earth!

The disciples **BUSTED** right up out of religion, what they had been taught, what they knew about life, ministry, Jesus, family, responsibility, accountability, and even what they knew about the marketplace, right on into a new fivefold paradigm. Consider the instance when Peter, James, and John, the sons of Zebedee had fished all day in their regular jobs and caught nothing. Jesus told them exactly where to cast their nets – into the deep - so abundance could SHIFT upon their destiny and calling. It caused a domino effect! Launching into the deep was a prophetic act of the SHIFT that was about to take place in them. They were so in awe of how honoring Jesus' word brought fruit that Peter bowed in reverence and he and his partners forsook all and followed Jesus.

<u>Forsook</u> in the Greek is *aphiēmi* and *hiēmi* and means:
1. (to send; an intensive form of *eimi*, to go)
2. to send forth, in various applications (as follow)
3. cry, forgive, forsake, lay aside, leave, let (alone, be, go, have)
4. omit, put (send) away, remit, suffer, yield up
5. to send away, to bid going away or depart, of a husband divorcing his wife
6. to send forth, yield up, to expire, to let go, let alone, let be
7. to disregard, to leave, not to discuss now, to neglect
8. to leave, go way from one in order to go to another place, to depart from any one

9. to depart from one and leave him to himself so that all mutual claims are abandoned
10. to desert wrongfully, to go away leaving something behind
11. to leave one by not taking him as a companion, to leave on dying
12. leave behind one, to leave so that what is left may remain, leave remaining
13. abandon, leave destitute

Members must have a mind of divorcing everything to BUST out of the four walls of the church into fivefold ministry. This will appear to be a one-sided divorce, yet it is essential to know that we all must choose the Lord for ourselves.

I was searching God for the reason SHIFTING into fivefold ministry posed such a SUDDENLY, and the Lord said the fivefold ministry is not a passive or pacifying ministry. It is an active, progressive and evolving ministry. Fivefold ministry is hands-on training and hands-on living. Though equipping is essential, the set time for SHIFTING into it is Jesus' timing. Though there is a lifestyle of training, equipping and releasing, the ministry begins when God says the SHIFT is now. It is not determined by whether we think we are ready or can handle it, but by who God choses and decides he wants to use, who he decides is ready, and who is willing to SHIFT with him. Today I just want to encourage you the called-out SHIFTERS – the called-out fivefold vision carriers. May you know God handpicked you and this perfect time to plant for his glory. **SHIFT!**

> ***Romans 8:30*** *Moreover whom he did predestinate, them he also called: and whom he called, them he also justified: and whom he justified, them he also glorified.*

The walls will try to keep you inside. The walls will come up with all kinds of reasons why what you are doing is enough and why change is not necessary. The "suddenly" SHIFT will assist you with SHIFTING out of the walls into the purpose and momentum of God. My ministry never had a traditional church paradigm. Yet it has taken a conscious effort not to succumb to the four walls of the church. Especially initially starting as a house ministry where many people rejected the vision because it is was small, intimate, developing, and lacked the bells and whistles of a traditional church paradigm. Some of the ways my ministry has resisted the four walls of the church and have remained true to fivefold ministry are as follows:

- Train everyone in their destiny and calling and assisted them with releasing their own fivefold vision. Have services and events related to these visions. The vision carriers in my ministry have businesses, production company, apparel company, fellowship ministry, so much of what we do is a nontraditional service or event.

- Place everyone on a ministry track so they would have areas to study and work on with God even when we did not have services.
- Only had Sunday services and any other service and event as God leads.
- Used Sunday service time for training, equipping, and fellowship.
- Have times of fellowship and team and member building rather than tradition Sunday services and other services. Sometimes we go places like the movies, mall, dinner, etc. We make it a point to evangelize while we are out in the community during these fellowship times. It is great to go shopping and require everyone to pray for two people before we all leave. Great way to reach the lost.
- Evangelize on Sundays and other days rather than have services.
- Partner with other ministries, attend their ministries on Sunday, and help them establish areas of fivefold ministry, e.g. dance ministry, atmospheric worship, deliverance ministry, altar workers ministry, prophetic ministry.
- Volunteer at various community events.
- Volunteer at shelters and prisons.
- Attend business classes, social service, and political meetings during the week, and then rest on Sundays.
- Conduct services and events on other days of the week then rest on Sundays.
- Pray on Sundays via conference call rather than have traditional services.
- Have trainings and equipping on Sundays via the internet rather than have traditional Sunday services.
- Conduct ministry abroad and take as many of our team and members as possible.
- Travel abroad for training and equipping, taking as many of our team and members as possible.
- Travel abroad as a team and ministry for times of refreshing and covenant bonding.
- Developing a culture that ministry is every day. I encourage my team and members to evangelize and minister to as many people as possible every day. They can do this via text message, phone, social media, on their job, school, while they are out and about. They are trained and equipped in the compassion of Jesus Christ, discernment, prayer, prophecy, exhortation, words of knowledge, wisdom, counsel, and revelation so they can witness effectively.
- Not allow others to interject traditional church services upon us as it is not our vision.
- Cultivate a healthy identity where we are confident and grounded with what God has called us to and not allow the fact that others may not understand it, value it, or speak against it, make us feel we are less than or noneffective in the kingdom.

One of the most challenging factors many have is making destiny with Jesus a lifestyle and not a thing to do on Sundays, Wednesdays, and other days they attend church programs. The BUSTING OUT lifestyle is a daily routine that makes EVERY decision through the covenant relationship with God. That includes:

- ✓ What to do with time;
- ✓ Consideration of how marriage is impacted by this SHIFT. What role do they have with aligning the marriage to the fivefold paradigm;
- ✓ What children can do that may impact their time;
- ✓ What lifestyle and activities their children engage in that draws them into a destiny lifestyle;
- ✓ What life activities they engage in;
- ✓ When and how they give God time (consistency);
- ✓ When they engage in godly activities as there is recognition that there is always something to do for God;
- ✓ Where they work, attend school, what purpose and impact they have at work and school;
- ✓ Whether they work for the world and infiltrate those systems, or they work for themselves and build godly systems;
- ✓ Where they go, even Christian circles. Do these places have purpose, edify God, empower the God in them;
- ✓ How they engage relationships, even family and loved ones; how these relationships impact their ability to remain true to the standards of God.

On and on these considerations go. It is no longer getting God in when you can, choosing soccer over Bible study or Sunday Services, going to work to make money or to pay bills rather than to church. But God truly becomes the center and head of your life, and everything truly is filtered through him! AND I MEAN EVERYTHING! For SHIFTING into a fivefold ministry vision yields a new perspective to "my life is not my own." Even if you are at soccer or work, you know it is because you have purpose there, as otherwise it will not be part of your life – it is a buried activity of the old life because it lacks destiny purpose. This paragraph may seem like extremism, but trust me, in time, you will process life through the Spirit of God as easily as breathing without giving it any thought. Be willing to pay the price for the SHIFT. Will it cost? Yes! Will it be worth it? Yes! It will be a bargain!

After suddenly SHIFTING with God, this is where the process of understanding what true fivefold ministry begins. This is where choices to choose God's plan over EVERYTHING will have to be made.

- Your flesh will not like this process.
- Your mind, will, heart, and emotions will not like this process.
- At times, you will not like this process.

- Your family, spouses, children, friends, and acquaintances may not like this process.
- Whomever benefited from who you used to be will not like this process.
- Devils, especially familiar spirits and generational strongholds, and destiny killing spirits, will definitely not like this process. They prefer the old you!

As you surrender and see the fruit of destiny versus church as usual, you will fall in love with this new SHIFT. It will feel like your own identity and what you knew about God, yourself, life, church, and ministry has died. Believe me those things have died! It has experienced a death on the cross and will now arise in true fivefold resurrection life with Jesus Christ. SHIFT! SHIFT RIGHT NOW! SHIFT!

Homework Explorations

1. Journal your revelation concerning this chapter.
2. How do you handle suddenly SHIFTS?
3. What areas of your emotions, character, and obedience do you need to improve in the handle suddenly SHIFTS?
4. Study the definition of the word "forsook." Journal revelation of how the disciples had to forsake all to SHIFT with God. Journal what God is requiring of you to forsake to SHIFT with God?
5. Journal your death process as you are SHIFTING to doing Jesus as a destiny lifestyle.

Taking Mountains

You may have heard charismatic ministers refer to the seven mountains. The mountains they speak of are the world systems that many believe we are to infiltrate and overtake. They are as follows:

1. Government
2. Media
3. Arts and entertainment
4. Business
5. Education
6. Religion
7. Family and generations

Though infiltrating and overtaking these mountains is beneficial, I believe as fivefold leaders, especially fivefold officers, we are to establish our own mountains and draw souls away from the world and demonic systems to God's kingdom. The world system is full of policies and laws that are contrary to standards of God. They are full of perversion, idolatry, pride, and self-exaltation of which laws are created to justify the freedom to make godless choices. We need more Christian lawmakers. We do not have enough kingdom influence within the government arena to SHIFT laws to godly standards where we can sufficiently make an impact throughout world systems. We have constitutional rights to freedom of speech and to serve our God – the Lord and Savior Jesus Christ; therefore, as we create our own ministry, businesses, organizations, entertainment, and other venues, we can implement godly standards. Those who come to the mountains we have built be kingdom standards will be expected to respect and abide by godly standards.

> **Revelations 11:15** *And the seventh angel sounded; and there were great voices in heaven, saying, the kingdoms of this world are become the kingdoms of our Lord, and of his Christ; and he shall reign for ever and ever.*

> **The Amplified Bible** *The seventh angel then blew [his] trumpet, and there were mighty voices in heaven, shouting, The dominion (kingdom, sovereignty, rule) of the world has now come into the possession and become the kingdom of our Lord and of His Christ (the Messiah), and He shall reign forever and ever (for the eternities of the eternities)!*

There are demonic system that we are to totally annihilate. Demonic systems consist of principalities, territorial spirits, powers, rulers of darkness, spiritual wickedness in high places.

> ***Ephesians 6:12*** *For we wrestle not against flesh and blood, but against principalities, against powers, against the rulers of the darkness of this world, against spiritual wickedness in high places.*

Apostle Paul

In Acts 16:25-26, Apostle Paul not only infiltrated and overtook the mountain of Delphi, but he supernaturally destroyed its entire prison system with a praise and worship earthquake that he and Silas released from jail.

> ***Acts 16:16-19*** *And it came to pass, as we went to prayer, a certain damsel possessed with a spirit of divination met us, which brought her masters much gain by soothsaying: The same followed Paul and us, and cried, saying, These men are the servants of the most high God, which shew unto us the way of salvation. And this did she many days. But Paul, being grieved, turned and said to the spirit, I command thee in the name of Jesus Christ to come out of her. And he came out the same hour.*

This damsel appeared to be for Paul and the other believers, but in actuality, she was attempting false persuasion so people would continue to come to her for soothsaying. She worked as a diviner for the region of Delphi. She set upon its famous oracle seat and people paid her to release witchcraft on their behalf.

The word divination in this scripture is the word *pytho* meaning *python*. In Greek mythology the name of the Pythian serpent or dragon that dwelt in the region of *Pytho* at the foot of Parnassus in Phocis and was said to have guarded the oracle at Delphi and been slain by Apolloa spirit of divination.

Paul was weary of her efforts to be familiar with them, and he turned to cast the python spirit out of her. Some believers say a person cannot have a principality demon, but this woman had one. She divined for the REGION of Delphi. She was a territorial principality in a human body. Her deliverance caused so much ruckus because of her position and ability to make money for the regional powers that Paul and Silas were jailed.

And when her masters saw that the hope of their gains was gone, they caught Paul and Silas, and drew them into the marketplace to answer to the local rulers.

Acts 16:19-26 (The Message)

19-22 When her owners saw that their lucrative little business was suddenly bankrupt, they went after Paul and Silas, roughed them up and dragged them into the market square. Then the police arrested them and pulled them into a court with the accusation, "These men are disturbing the peace—dangerous Jewish agitators subverting our Roman law and order." By this time the crowd had turned into a restless mob out for blood.

22-24 The judges went along with the mob, had Paul and Silas's clothes ripped off and ordered a public beating. After beating them black-and-blue, they threw them into jail, telling the jailkeeper to put them under heavy guard so there would be no chance of escape. He did just that—threw them into the maximum security cell in the jail and clamped leg irons on them.

25-26 Along about midnight, Paul and Silas were at prayer and singing a robust hymn to God. The other prisoners couldn't believe their ears. Then, without warning, a huge earthquake! The jailhouse tottered, every door flew open, all the prisoners were loose.

Acts 16:27-34 (The Message)

27-28 Startled from sleep, the jailer saw all the doors swinging loose on their hinges. Assuming that all the prisoners had escaped, he pulled out his sword and was about to do himself in, figuring he was as good as dead anyway, when Paul stopped him: "Don't do that! We're all still here! Nobody's run away!"

29-31 The jailer got a torch and ran inside. Badly shaken, he collapsed in front of Paul and Silas. He led them out of the jail and asked, "Sirs, what do I have to do to be saved, to really live?" They said, "Put your entire trust in the Master Jesus. Then you'll live as you were meant to live—and everyone in your house included!"

32-34 They went on to spell out in detail the story of the Master—the entire family got in on this part. They never did get to bed that night. The jailer made them feel at home, dressed their wounds, and then—he couldn't wait till morning!—was baptized, he and everyone in his family. There in his home, he had food set out for a festive meal. It was a night to remember: He and his entire family had put their trust in God; everyone in the house was in on the celebration.

While in jail, Paul and Silas released such earth shattering praises that the FOUNDATION - the false institutional system - of the prison shook, the prison doors open, and the shackles were loosed. Total uprooting from its core and deliverance from the bondages of this demonic system manifested, such that the guard almost killed himself for fearing the prisoners had fled. The guard sought salvation for him and his family after witnessing this supernatural liberation. This is the level of regional judging praise that should be released from our fivefold ministry events and services.

Paul and Silas released such earth-shattering praise that the FOUNDATION – the institutional system – was shaken, doors opened, and shackles loosed.

If you read further you will find that Paul and Silas's praise reformation earthquake was a prophetic act, as after it happened, the magistrates agreed to privately release them. Paul demanded they be released openly by the magistrates. He was making sure all knew the mountain of Jesus had completely overridden the mountain of Delphi.

> **Verse 37-41** *But Paul said unto them, They have beaten us openly uncondemned, being Romans, and have cast us into prison; and now do they thrust us out privily? nay verily; but let them come themselves and fetch us out. And the serjeants told these words unto the magistrates: and they feared, when they heard that they were Romans. And they came and besought them, and brought them out, and desired them to depart out of the city. And they went out of the prison, and entered into the house of Lydia: and when they had seen the brethren, they comforted them, and departed.*

<u>Jesus Christ</u>

Jesus, the Chief Apostle not only infiltrated and overtook the mountain of Satan, he descended to hell, took the keys of death and hell, thus destroying death's mountain. Keys denotes gatekeeping, power, and authority. Jesus made it clear that he now owned all the earth and he alone held the power over life and death. Jesus established the heavenly mountain of life and established fivefold ministry.

> **Revelation 1:18** *I am he that liveth, and was dead; and, behold, I am alive for evermore, Amen; and have the keys of hell and of death.*

> **Ephesians 4:8** *But unto every one of us is given grace according to the measure of the gift of Christ. Wherefore he saith, When he ascended up on high, he led captivity captive, and gave gifts unto men. (Now that he ascended, what is it but that he also descended first into the lower parts of the earth? He that descended is the same also that ascended up far above all heavens, that he might fill all things.). And he gave some, apostles; and some, prophets; and some, evangelists; and some, pastors and teachers;*

Apostle Peter

Apostle Peter was to be a literal mountain to which Jesus built his church so that the gates of hell could not prevail against it. His mandate was to shut up gateways of hell in people's lives, generations, lands, cites, regions, and spheres, such that hell could not influence, predominate, or advance in the earth.

> *Matthew 16:18* And I say also unto thee, That thou art Peter, and upon this rock I will build my church; and the gates of hell shall not prevail against it.

The purpose of destroying mountains is to pull down strongholds and high places, judge witches, warlocks, demonic rulers, annihilate their idolatry, witchcraft, and demonic powers, and establish the kingdom of God as a replacement of those forces.

We are to contend against these worldly and demonic systems by demolishing and displacing darkness and wickedness. We should be gatekeepers of lands, regions, and spheres, while opposing witchcraft, satanism, idolatry, demonic high places and covens, demonic cultures and trends, demonic ideologies, laws, and falsehoods, demonic religious counterfeits, and hell itself.

It is important to govern your mountain once you establish it. In *1Kings 18-22*, we find Elijah not only infiltrating and overtaking Jezebel's mountain, but he destroyed her mountain. It angered her so intensely that she threatened Elijah's life. Because he ran due to her threats, Elijah left his mountain vulnerable and exposed. His departure left Jezebel and her husband Ahab alive. Elijah had to return in order that the events that would kill them both could unfold. He had to reestablish and solidify his mountain. God had to strengthen and refocus the prophet. After he was strengthened upon the mountain of God, Elijah gathered his troops and returned to finish the kingdom work that was his assignment, including a succession plan for Elisha to receive his mantle.

When we take over and establish godly mountains, we establish regional reformation through our fivefold vision. Our vision SHIFTS outside the four walls of the ministry and challenges demonic and world systems and their demonic forces. It also declares the Lordship of Jesus Christ, establishes that there is no God but Jesus, unveils the victory of the cross, restores the people and region to God, and creates a mountain for him to draw souls and get glory.

As fivefold ministers and ministries, you must want your mountains. So many want the title, and to do the work in the safety of the church but have not learned to want their mountains. You are not experiencing the fullness of your destiny and calling until you take your mountains. The kingdom of God is not fully being established in you until you take your mountains. The kingdom of hell is prevailing when we do not take over our mountains.

Taking mountains is also about overtaking land and territory. Go after the demon forces for God has given you victory to recover all. SHIFT!

> ***1Samuel 30:8*** *And David enquired at the Lord, saying, Shall I pursue after this troop? shall I overtake them? And he answered him, Pursue: for thou shalt surely overtake them, and without fail recover all.*
>
> ***The Message Bible*** *The answer came, "Go after them! Yes, you'll catch them! Yes, you'll make the rescue!"*

Dictionary.com defines *infiltrate* as:
1. to filter into or through; permeate
2. to cause to pass in by filtering
3. to move into (an organization, country, territory, or the like) surreptitiously and gradually, especially with hostile intent
4. to pass a small number of (soldiers, spies, or the like) into a territory or organization clandestinely and with hostile or subversive intent

Dictionary.com defines *overtake* as:
1. to catch up with in traveling or pursuit; draw even with
2. to catch up with and pass, as in a race; move by
3. to move ahead of in achievement, production, score, etc.; surpass
4. to happen to or befall someone suddenly or unexpectedly, as night, a storm, or death
5. to pass another vehicle

Dictionary.com defines *recover* as:
1. to get back or regain (something lost or taken away): to recover a stolen watch.
2. to make up for or make good (loss, damage, etc., to oneself)
3. to regain the strength, composure, balance, or the like, of (oneself)
4. Law.
    a. to obtain by judgment in a court of law, or by legal proceedings: to recover damages for a wrong.
    b. to acquire title to through judicial process: to recover land.
5. to reclaim from a bad state, practice, etc.
6. to regain (a substance) in usable form, as from refuse material or from a waste product or by-product of manufacture; reclaim
7. Military. to return (a weapon) to a previously held position in the manual of arms

8. Football. to gain or regain possession of (a fumble)
9. to regain health after being sick, wounded, or the like (often followed by from)
10. to regain a former and better state or condition
11. to regain one's strength, composure, balance, etc.
12. Law. to obtain a favorable judgment in a suit for something
13. to make a recovery in fencing or rowing

There is land and territory that is on the blueprint God has trusted to you! Come on and take your mountain. SHIFT!

1Samuel 30:18-19 *And David recovered all that the Amalekites had carried away: and David rescued his two wives. And there was nothing lacking to them, neither small nor great, neither sons nor daughters, neither spoil, nor any thing that they had taken to them: David recovered all.*

Habakkuk 3:19 *The Lord GOD is my strength, And He has made my feet like hinds' feet, And makes me walk on my high places. For the choir director, on my stringed instruments.*

Deuteronomy 32:13 *"He made him ride on the high places of the earth, And he ate the produce of the field; And He made him suck honey from the rock, And oil from the flinty rock,*

Psalms 18:33 *He makes my feet like hinds' feet, And sets me upon my high places.*

2Samuel 22:34 *He makes my feet like hinds' feet, And sets me on my high places.*

How to Take Mountains:

- You take mountains in prayer. You search God for revelation regarding the principalities, powers and demonic forces that currently have your mountains or that are coming against your mountains. You consistently wage war in prayer to apostolically dismantle and displace their ownership, presence, and authority over the people, land, and atmosphere of that mountain. In engaging in apostolic warfare, you are asserting God's authority and kingdom over the authority kingdom of darkness.

Job 22:28 8 *Thou shalt also decree a thing, and it shall be established unto thee: and the light shall shine upon thy ways.*

- You consistently pray, praise and worship at events, services, gatherings, and in your private time to prophetically disrupt and uproot the demonic foundational systems, protocols, wrongdoings, and bondages of your mountains.

    Psalms 100:4 *Enter into his gates (heavenlies) with thanksgiving, and into his courts (throne room) with praise (exaltation): be thankful (adoration) unto him, and bless his name.*

    As you praise, the gates of heaven are opened to you and you are postured inside the court room - the throne room of heaven. Gates represent access and courts represent judgement and justice being released. Your praise of God and unto God is releasing filling up your life, generations, situations, regions, spheres, nations, climates, frequencies, airways, with the truth of who God is and the truth of his identity is releasing judgment and justice on your behalf. This is the reason an earthquake occurred as Paul and Silas prayed and praised in the jail in **Acts 16**. Judgement and justice were being released from their jurisdiction, to the demonic system that was holding them captive. Be sure to send your praises, decrees, judgements to these mountains and call out these demonic principalities, powers, etc., by name so that your workings can leave your jurisdiction and infiltrate these spheres to dismantle and displace these entities

    John 4:24 *God is Spirit, and those who worship Him must worship in spirit and truth.*

- You pray and get strategy from God of how to physically infiltrate systems and literally go to these mountains and overthrow darkness; while also establishing God's mountain in that sphere.

    Mark 16:15 *And He said to them, "Go into all the world and preach the gospel to every creature.*

    You have to go into the educational system, media system, political system, businesses system, etc. and physically tread with the souls of your feet, while implementing God's plan of recovery and dominion. You do this by planting yourself through job and volunteer positions. You can also plant a mountain by starting your own organizations, service agencies, schools, colleges, hospitals, banks, businesses, mandates, programs, etc.

    Mark 13:7-11 *And when ye shall hear of wars and rumours of wars, be ye not troubled: for such things must needs be; but the end shall not be yet. For nation shall rise against nation, and kingdom against kingdom: and there shall be earthquakes in divers places, and there shall be famines and troubles: these are the beginnings of* *sorrows. But take heed to yourselves: for they shall deliver you up to councils; and in the synagogues ye shall be beaten: and ye shall be brought before rulers and kings for my sake, for a testimony against them. And the gospel must first be published among all nations. But when they shall lead you, and deliver you up, take no thought beforehand what ye shall speak, neither do ye premeditate: but whatsoever shall be given you in that hour, that speak ye: for it is not ye that speak, but the Holy Ghost.*

Even if God leads you to plant a church, hub, equipping center, make sure the vision entails pursuing, overtaking, and recovering land, community, the airways and frequencies, the heavenlies, and the region. I believe churches were not meant just for the purposes of assembling believers. They were meant to serve as godly mountains in communities and regions. Churches are godly high places for people to come and glorify the King of kings and Lord of lords.

Infiltration Decree
I decree you shall infiltrate strategic areas, arenas, and spheres and claim your mountains. I decree you shall overtake simply by your bold presence. I decree you shall be focused in consuming that area - that sphere with God's glory and recover all. I decree you shall recover all God has ordained for you. Nothing will be lost, denied, stifled, or left behind. You shall infiltrate, overtake and recover all. Know that this word is from the Lord for you and goes before you. Go in expectation, expecting to plunder and overtake. Expect to receive all God has for you in every season. Victory is designed and evident for your mounts are yours says the Lord. SHIFT!

Homework Explorations
1. Journal your thoughts on this chapter.
2. Study the story of Elijah in **1Kings 18-24**. Write a two page paper on his journey of overthrown Jezebel's mountain, running, then returning to reestablish the mountain of God.
3. Journal in detail on how your fivefold ministry need to infiltrate mountains. Journal on all three stages.
4. Study **Mark 13:7-11**. Journal how this applies to your destiny and calling.

Contending Against Principalities and Powers

As you begin to vision cast (activate your vision), train, and equip, and as you SHIFT into seasons of planting, plowing, and building, the region will begin to respond to the manifestations of the sons of God SHIFTING into their rightful place in the earth.

> **Romans 8:18-19** *For I reckon that the sufferings of this present time are not worthy to be compared with the glory which shall be revealed in us. For the earnest expectation of the creature waiteth for the manifestation of the sons of God.*

Manifestation means to *reveal, come forth, lay bare, reveal, make naked*. You and the vision carriers – the sons of God – are actually being exposed and the region is responding to your identity, destiny, and calling in the earth.

The principalities, territorial spirits, and powers of that region are also being made aware of your manifestation. They will arise to contend against you and the vision because you are delivering that territory. Demonic forces do not want to give up their rule. The principalities and territorial spirits will send watcher spirits, scanner spirits, ease dropping spirits, demonic trackers, to scout you and to scout out the vision. They will seek to counterattack. The squatter spirits that have lived on the land or in the realms that you are now going after will report to demonic camps and witchcraft covens regarding your work and will commit to counterattacking for rule of the land, buildings, spiritual realms, and spheres.

Witches and warlocks are offensive, so you may rest assured that there has already been a release of demonic forces against believers and ministries of the region. They are disciplined in spending consistent time demonically praying and interjecting spells and workings into the stars, moon, sun, land, airways, frequencies, to influence and attack believers. They are already vigilant in translating in and out of the spirit realm and spying out the land concerning the workings of believers and ministries. Witches and warlocks will visit the physical homes, lands, services and events of believers and release spells and witchcraft workings. They will infiltrate teams and events to gain intel and to contaminate and stifle the vision. Demonic spirits are making full use of the internet and technology, so they are even more effective in stifling any vision that would try to come forth. That should not deter those who may already have reservations about using technology. Quite the contrary, it should encourage us to take dominion over the airways. Witches and warlocks often govern the airways and spiritual realms of regions. Just think about various television shows that are rooted in sexual perversion and idolatry. Those are the ones that the secular world applauds and awards with Emmys and Oscars and other awards. They also own land where their businesses and money operations occur. In addition, they are busy saturating political and economic arenas to instill laws and systems that promote their agenda in the earth. They love to influence the political and educational arenas so they can impact the decisions and ideologies of people and generations. As you release your vision, expect to contend against witchcraft that has already been released in your region, released specifically against the saints, and the witchcraft that will be released as the demonic agents make the witches and warlocks aware of you taking your rightful place in the earth. Remember that it is not a fearful warfare for the believer as we have already conquered through the death, burial, and resurrection of Jesus Christ.

> ***Deuteronomy 18:10-16*** *There shall not be found among you any one that maketh his son or his daughter to pass through the fire, or that useth divination, or an observer of times, or an enchanter, or a witch, Or a charmer, or a consulter with familiar spirits, or a wizard, or a necromancer. For all that do these things are an abomination unto the Lord: and because of these abominations the Lord thy God doth drive them out from before thee. Thou shalt be perfect with the Lord thy God. For these nations, which thou shalt possess, hearkened unto observers of times, and unto diviners: but as for thee, the Lord thy God hath not suffered thee so to do. The Lord thy God will raise up unto thee a Prophet from the midst of thee, of thy brethren, like unto me; unto him ye shall hearken;*
>
> ***Micah 5:10-15*** *And it shall come to pass in that day, saith the Lord, that I will cut off thy horses out of the midst of thee, and I will destroy thy chariots: And I will cut off the cities of thy land, and throw down all thy strong holds: And I will cut off witchcrafts out of thine hand; and thou shalt have no more soothsayers: Thy graven images also will I cut off, and thy standing images out of the midst of thee;*
> *and thou shalt no more worship the work of thine hands. And I will pluck up thy groves out of the midst of thee: so will I destroy thy cities. And I will execute vengeance in anger and fury upon the heathen,*
> *such as they have not heard.*
>
> ***Revelations 18:23-24*** *And the light of a candle shall shine no more at all in thee; and the voice of the bridegroom and of the bride shall be heard no more at all in thee for thy merchants were the great men of the earth; for by thy sorceries were all nations deceived. And in her was found the blood of prophets, and of saints, and of all that were slain upon the earth.*

The vision carriers, fivefold officers, and even the members will become increasing aware of the demonic forces in the region. This is because the eyes of your understanding are being enlightened to the opposition of your vision.

> ***Ephesians 1:18*** *The eyes of your understanding being enlightened; that ye may know what is the hope of his calling, and what the riches of the glory of his inheritance in the saints.*

Hopefully, it is becoming clear to you that you are not just evolving in destiny or establishing a kingdom vision, but you are taking up dominion in the earth. In order to have dominion, you must take authority over every living thing that creeps in your sphere of influence. It will require a spiritual battle against principalities, territorial spirit, and powers to assert your dominion in the earth.

These entities will send psychological and mental warfare as an attempt to confound and stifle your work and progress. The psychological and mental warfare may feel heavy around you. Psychological warfare is meant to weary and wear you down. This is not a 21st century phenomenon as Daniel spoke of the same dynamic. In fact, he was prophesying that this would come as part of the end times. Is it any wonder that our society is so plagued with afflictions of the mind, e.g. depression, anxiety, and so on?

> ***Daniel 7:25*** *And he shall speak great words against the most High, and shall wear out the saints of the most High, and think to change times and laws: and they shall be given into his hand until a time and times and the dividing of time.*

The demonic forces that are unleashed in our time will attack like a throbbing headache that simply will not go away. Over and over, there is a pounding that hell has unleashed in hopes of spiritually exhausting the warriors of the Lord's kingdom. Those spirits will try to resurface old sin patterns and crack open closed doors and make you think you are not equipped or prepared for what God has granted your hands to do. They will try to get you focused on searching yourself for sin issues when there are no open doors in your life. The effort is to get you self-absorbed which pulls your focus away from being empowered by the Spirit and striving to do the work through will power.

People will stir psychological and mental warfare around you regarding the vision.

- ➢ Some of these people will lack understanding of the vision and will speak against it.
- ➢ Some serve as demonic powers in the region and are coming against you as an influencer of the region.
- ➢ Some will be family members that are stirred by destiny killing spirits and familiar spirits in your family line. They will use these family members to attack you.
- ➢ Some will be saints and ministries who feel threatened by your vision. You will want them to celebrate you as an expansion of the kingdom in the

region, but the Saul spirit will use them to throw javelins at you and the vision.
- ➢ Some will be innocent people being used ignorantly by the devil to contend against you and the vision. Situations will use pop off for no apparent reason to distract, weary, delay, and murder the vision.

Their words are released to plant seeds of doubt, fear, worry, insecurity death, or to curse you and the vision. It is important to know your identity, authority, and clarity regarding your calling and the vision, so you can combat and snuff out these words and mental interjections quickly. Do you remember when Peter was rebuked by Jesus?

> *Mark 8:33 But when He had turned around and looked at His disciples, He rebuked Peter, saying, "Get behind Me, Satan! For you are not mindful of the things of God, but the things of men."*

Jesus was not telling Peter to go away forever. He did not remove Peter from his team. What he was strong enough to do is to tell Peter, "I cannot have you walking beside me right now, because you are not lined up to what God has told me to do." In some instances, we have to own the destiny assignment that God has given to tell people who have been close to us for years, "I can't let you be in my ear right now." We must know the vision and own the strategy!

The python spirit will often manifest when you begin planting and when you are starting new works. The python spirit also comes to snuff out revival fire and revival reformation. The python spirit wraps itself around the region, the vision, the vision carriers, and the ministry, and squeeze the fire, praise, joy, zeal, and life out of it. It will release depression, heaviness, apathy, sluggardness, while slowly squeezing the strength, power, revival, and breath until there is no life. It will also weigh down and press down and make it difficult to embrace the day, complete tasks, carry the vision and call that is upon one's life. Praise, worship, and releasing the revival fire, and vengeful fire of the Lord are all essential to opposing and displacing the python spirit.

It is important to communicate as a team regarding the warfare that each team member is experiencing as often part of the strategy is to individuals believe they are the only one battling. Demons will use this lie to isolate teammates and oppress them while placing more pressure on them to quit.

Make communication a foundational requirement for team members! Be completely transparent with one another so that the devil cannot isolate any of your team.

Make communication a foundational requirement for vision carriers and team members, and the ministry so destiny cannot be aborted, or visions stifled and delayed because people are overwhelmed by unnecessary warfare. Warfare is part of the vision and comes with the territory but remember that we are MORE than conquerors. The vision is for the purposes of overthrowing darkness and becoming a light. Contention is to be expected and even welcomed. I say welcomed because the more you are aware of darkness in your region, the greater you will be as a force that can dismantle it for God's glory.

Rest and a balanced lifestyle are very important as you are releasing the vision. The enemy loves to hit with colds, sinus infections, flus, viruses, stomach problems, afflictions, illnesses, demonic dreams and deposits, especially when vision carriers are tired and overwhelmed. It is best to take time to rest when you find yourself stressed. Did you catch "when" and not "if"? Discern when rest is needed or when afflictions from tiredness are trying to attack. It is better to take time out for a couple of days than to have to take a week or two off due to being ill from a lack of rest. The body will take a longer time to recover than it would if you were just taking a moment to recoup. Stay balanced in carrying the vision.

In addition, it is important to have rest days built into your week where you can take one day a week just for yourself. This day is for you to do nothing if you want, watch tv, read a book, shop, hang with family or friends **BUT NOT DO MINISTRY**. Spend time refreshing in the presence of the Lord. Your personal day needs to be a set day every week where everyone knows this is your day. You are off limits. Having it as a set day also adds discipline to rest becoming a lifestyle and where boundaries are established. Place a mature leader in charge so that members can reach out in case of emergencies. Part of that plan is teaching your members how to go to God first. It is setting a healthy example for your entire ministry when the leader has boundaries. In a growing ministry, there will always be members in various stages of maturity. Some are still learning the meaning of a true emergency versus trying to get you to be God. That is not a criticism of the individual but a simple truth for a growing body of believers. When leaders do not have boundaries, they will begin operating in a fixer spirit, rescuing spirit, false obligations, or a pastoral paradigm. When I take my personal day and especially when I recognize that I am tired, I sleep, rest, and spending time soaking in the presence of God. I will sleep soak where I will spend the day focusing on communing with the Holy Spirit and allowing myself to sleep inside the glory of God.

As I am taking deep breaths to release tension and SHIFT myself in a relaxing inside the Holy Spirit,
- I will praise and worship to open the heavenlies and call for the glory to consume my home to set the atmosphere for divine encounters with God.

- I send angels to deal with any darkness or warfare and I remain focused on communing and surrendering to God. I focused on being with him and him ministering to me and me ministering to him.
- I focus on scriptures, or a character, fruit of the spirit, desire, or attribute of God I want to be empowered in and ask the Holy Spirit to fill me with it. For example, I may want to experience more of the love of God or to be filled with the love of God, so I will focus on scriptures regarding this fruit or focus on communing with the Holy Spirit empowering me with this fruit and allow him to fill me with it.
- I may focus on resting at the feet of Jesus, laying on his bosom as I quietly praise and worship. This usually draws me into encounters with God, his heart, his presence and heaven.
- I may ask God to bring me to heaven to spend time with him, seeing and engaging in the rooms and courts of heaven. I spend time worshipping and resting and allowing God to ascend me to where he wants to take me. I usually fall into a deep sleep or a deep resting place and the Holy Spirit will SHIFT me into areas that God wants me to experience.

If I continue to be drawn into thinking about people or tasks, I will spend time breaking ungodly soul ties with people, life, ministry duties and anywhere I have taken on false obligations, false roles, become more than I should to people and where my gifts are operating through my heart rather than my spirit. The operation of spiritual gifts should not be dictating our momentum and flow with God. They should be subject to God and his spirit in us in the same way our soul, heart, flesh, and mind are subject to our spirit. Anytime we are in a place where we cannot rest or think we must be at the beck and call of everything and everyone else, we are imbalanced. When we cannot take a day to rest or even as we rest, responsibilities override our ability to rest, our gifts have become exalted above God's spirit. Spending time breaking ungodly soul ties is essential to casting down these thoughts. Learn to break strongholds with false burdens and obligations. Go back to the scripture where Jesus rebuked Peter. If Jesus had listened to Peter, there would be no Calvary experience. Peter was speaking from his heart for Jesus and not out of deliberately intending to sabotage Jesus' destiny. Jesus was discerning enough to know that he could not operate out of his love for his friend, but he had to stay on the destiny path that was in front of him.

We all need to check ourselves and be willing to cleanse from any emotional or mental baggage that we have accumulated throughout the day or week. Spend time breaking anyway that your spiritual gifts have exalted above your spiritual assignment. Surrendering gifts to the subjection of the Holy Spirit is essential to being delivered from this where you can truly posture in a spirit of rest. You have to give up the need to do something beyond refreshing and/or beyond being with God and allowing him to replenish you. If you have not surrender to that level on your rest day and are constantly up doing things or feeling drawn to check on situations and people, then you truly have not yielded to a posture of rest. You are still in your leadership mode or even the fixer and rescuer mode and are lending a door for the enemy to hit you with burnout. When I find myself in this place, I keep utilizing the soaking tools above to SHIFT me back into a posture of rest. It truly takes a lifestyle practice of breaking your will, submitting your personality and lifestyle behaviors to God to truly enter realms of rest. Not being able to surrender in this fashion reveals that in many ways you are guiding and carrying your destiny rather than letting God be your guide.

> **Galatians 2:19** The Amplified Bible I have been crucified with Christ [in Him I have shared His crucifixion]; it is no longer I who live, but Christ (the Messiah) lives in me; and the life I now live in the body I live by faith in (by adherence to and reliance on and complete trust in) the Son of God, Who loved me and gave Himself up for me.

> **James 4:9** The Amplified Bible Humble yourselves [feeling very insignificant] in the presence of the Lord, and He will exalt you [He will lift you up and make your lives significant].

> **Mark 11:28** Come to Me, all you who labor and are heavy-laden and overburdened, and I will cause you to rest. [I will ease and relieve and refresh your souls.] Take My yoke upon you and learn of Me, for I am gentle (meek) and humble (lowly) in heart, and you will find rest (relief and ease and refreshment and recreation and blessed quiet) for your souls. For My yoke is wholesome (useful, good—not harsh, hard, sharp, or pressing, but comfortable, gracious, and pleasant), and My burden is light and easy to be borne.

A yoke is a wooden beam put on two animals to balance them so they can work together and carry their share of the load with balance. When you are trying to rest, you must be intentional with taking on the yoke of the Lord where you are coming into balance of carrying life, destiny, and the vision with him. If you are praying, worshipping, and resting, but still feel weighted then you have not fully surrendered where the yoke is balanced between you and God. You may need to cry out in a yearning where you tap into his presence until you are broken in a total surrendering to him. SHIFT into feasting on the pleasures of his glory. You may need to come into an understanding that the more you rest and live in God's presence, the more you radiate, produce, and release his glory – embody the literal essence of God's glory.

> **Deuteronomy 4:29** But from there you will seek the LORD your God, and you will find Him if you seek Him with all your heart and with all your soul. (**when you are**

resting to encounter God, you continuously seek him all day until you encounter him. You may have to keep entering into his presence while resting become idle, bored, focused on something else, yielding to something else. You break your will by continuing to make him your focus and pursuit).

Psalms 51:10-17 *Create in me a clean heart, O God, and renew a right, persevering, and steadfast spirit within me. Cast me not away from Your presence and take not Your Holy Spirit from me. Restore to me the joy of Your salvation and uphold me with a willing spirit. Then will I teach transgressors Your ways, and sinners shall be converted and return to You. Deliver me from bloodguiltiness and death, O God, the God of my salvation, and my tongue shall sing aloud of Your righteousness (Your rightness and Your justice). O Lord, open my lips, and my mouth shall show forth Your praise. You delight not in sacrifice, or else would I give it; You find no pleasure in burnt offering. My sacrifice [the sacrifice acceptable] to God is a broken spirit; a broken and a contrite heart [broken down with sorrow for sin and humbly and thoroughly penitent], such, O God, You will not despise.* (**On rest day, your sacrifice is yourself and everything that gets in the way of experiencing God.**

Psalms 16:11 *You will show me* (**visions, divine encounters**) *the path of life; In Your presence is fullness of joy; At Your right hand are pleasures forevermore.*

Psalms 100:2-5 *Serve the LORD with gladness; Come before His presence with singing. {3} Know that the LORD, He is God; It is He who has made us, and not we ourselves; We are His people and the sheep of His pasture. Enter into His gates with thanksgiving* (**heavenly gates, heavenly places**)*, And into His courts with praise* (**enter heavenly courts**)*. Be thankful to Him, and bless His name. For the LORD is good; His mercy is everlasting, And His truth endures to all generations.*

Psalms 34:8 *O taste and see that the Lord is good: blessed is the man that trusteth in him.* (**Feast on Jesus; digest him as you soak and consume his presence**).
Psalms 34:18-19 *The LORD is near to those who have a broken heart, And saves such as have a contrite spirit. Many are the afflictions of the righteous, But the LORD delivers him out of them all.* (**Break your will and be healed**)

James 4:8 *Draw near to God and He will draw near to you. Cleanse your hands, you sinners; and purify your hearts, you double-minded.* (**Drawing is an intentional pursuit; the more you draw the more you are able to be purged of stress, restlessness, restless thoughts that cause double mindedness**)

You may be wondering about the reasons I took time to speak about the topic of rest in the chapter regarding principalities, territorial spirits, and powers. It has been my observation that many leaders may not be guilty of blatant sin, but they are guilty of not resting, of operating in the fixer spirit, rescuing others, or carrying the vision in an imbalanced manner. It is the number one door opener to demonic hits.

Failing to include rest in your leadership plan is the number one door opener to unnecessary demonic hits.

It does not look like sin, but it is indeed sin because it is disobedience to rest. It is a rejection of balance. It is exalting ministry and life above God which is idolatry. It is denying your journey and momentum with the Lord. The enemy loves to hit when we are tired, weary and imbalanced. This is one of the main reasons that demons attack in our sleep and dreams. Our defenses are down so demons will come into the dream and sleep realm. These demonic sleep attacks will increase in weary times as the enemy will use them to plant demonic deposits and bring wrestling and restlessness in the sleep. Step by step, tiredness becomes weariness and weariness becomes exhaustion. I decree you are running with the valuable key to rest even as you run with the vision as it is a weapon against the enemy. SHIFT!

Let me take a moment to discuss demonic dream deposits. The night season is key for vision carriers. God gives a lot of strategies, revelations, and insight via dreams regarding the principalities, territorial spirits, and powers in the region. Often, we view these as nightmares and do not take time to interpret them. There is some nightmarish stuff going on in the high places, spirit realms, and dark alleys of your region. All kinds of evil dealings, demonic sacrifices, and debauchery is occurring. Do not get so caught up in releasing the vision where you create your own little world and do not annihilate darkness or lose focus concerning the saving of souls. What you establish should be an extension of heaven. People should view it as a safe place, a healing place, a deliverance place, and transformation edifice in the earth. As a matter of fact, **ask** God for dreams regarding your vision and region. Let God know that you want the inside scoop or what I like to call, the keys to breakthrough.

Even as you want the inside scoop, be mindful that demonic spirits attack vision carriers at night. They come through the dream or sleep realm to instill fear, insecurity, weariness, restlessness, grief, tragedy, lust, perversion, abortion, witchcraft, affliction, illness, disease, murder. They will attack the mind, heart, soul, body, reproductive and sexual organs, especially the womb. They will cause:

- Restless, demonic, sexually perverse, and ungodly dreams;
- Strangle, suffocate, physically attack you by beating on you, pulling out of bed, etc.;
- Plant demonic substances, fluids, use and insert objects in your body to extract and plant fluids and substances, violate your purity, cause affliction; Sometimes extracted are used on demonic items to release spells against you and the ministry, used as a point of contact to release hexes and vexes, or have devices for the purposes of telepathic communication – basically to spy or control you.

I know I just shocked or confirmed some experiences for some of you all, but what you are experiencing at night is real and ungodly. Remember that I have over 20 years' experience as a professional counselor and behavioral consultant, so this is not something I just made up for the sake of shock value. It is important to take authority over your night season by praying to shutdown demonic attacks at night, while declaring you sleep in the secret place with Jesus. I suggest that you consistently:

- Declare Psalms 91 out loud before going to bed.
- Close demonic portals in and around your home.
- Invite the angels to live at your home and to guard to gates of your dream and sleep realm.
- Release any stress and weights of the day to God before you go to sleep by cleansing yourself in the blood of Jesus and soaking in his glory as you drift off to sleep.
- Study David as he meditated frequently on his bed at night. He understood the importance of communing with God in his sleep and guarding his sleep realms.

Psalms 63:6 When I remember thee upon my bed, and meditate on thee in the night watches.

Psalms 1:2 But his delight is in the law of the LORD, and on His law he meditates day and night.

Psalms 16:7 I will bless the LORD who counsels me; even at night my conscience instructs me.

Psalms 42:8 The LORD decrees His loving devotion by day; and at night His song is with me--a prayer to the God of my life.

Psalms 119:148 My eyes anticipate the watches of night, that I may meditate on Your word.

> ***Psalms 130:6*** *My soul waits for the Lord more than watchmen for the morning-- more than watchmen waiting for the morning.*

Those who are in fivefold offices, especially the apostles and prophets who contend for regional reformation, will have experiences of ascending or translating to spiritual realms through their seat to deal with principalities and powers. This will occur when they war and intercede in prayer, preach, teach, complete various tasks to release the vision. They enter the second heavens where principalities and powers live and operate or may also ascend above into more authoritative heavenly realms. The ministry that is being conducted is casting down upon the demonic kingdoms. During these instances the fivefold officers are releasing the justice and judgments of the Lord where literally they are tearing down high places, demonic kingdoms, ideologies, and influences that have exalted itself against the truth and purposes of God.

> ***2Corinthians 10:3-6*** *For though we walk in the flesh, we do not war after the flesh: (For the weapons of our warfare are not carnal, but mighty through God to the pulling down of strong holds;) Casting down imaginations, and every high thing that exalteth itself against the knowledge of God, and bringing into captivity every thought to the obedience of Christ; And having in a readiness to revenge all disobedience, when your obedience is fulfilled.*

The demonic kingdom hates this infiltration and annihilation which is the reason they counterattack. They hate when fivefold officers ascend and infiltrate their spheres or ascend above them and strike their kingdom. They hate when we know we operate as holy principalities called to overthrow demonic principalities. They hate when we have entered a maturity in God where we tread and translate in spheres and realms. It is important to also note that we should be living and operating from these heavenly places as believers, but especially as fivefold officers.

> ***Ephesians 1:20*** *Which he wrought in Christ, when he raised him from the dead, and set him at his own right hand in the heavenly places,*

> ***Ephesians 2:6*** *And hath raised us up together, and made us sit together in heavenly places in Christ Jesus.*

As we learn to live in these realms, we begin to govern them because we have displaced demonic forces. Eventually there is less counterattack as we engage in these spheres. Until the full work in these reams is complete regarding displacing the demonic principalities or until you learn to live and govern in heavenly realms, it will be essential to release angels to further annihilate these demonic forces, close off gateways and portals once you complete a work in these realms, and cancel all backlash and vengeful assignments, as otherwise the demonic agents in these realms will track you and attack you with psychosocial, emotional, and physical warfare. You may not have to complete the work in one prayer session, event, or after completing a work or maybe you are the planter and someone else is to come along and water what you have begun. Be mindful to close yourself off from counterattacks and the demonic realm will counterattack with a vengeance. But this warfare can be deflected by canceling and guarding against it before it comes.

> ***Revelations 18:19-21*** *And they cast dust on their heads, and cried, weeping and wailing, saying, Alas, alas, that great city, wherein were made rich all that had ships in the sea by reason of her costliness! for in one hour is she made desolate. Rejoice over her, thou heaven, and ye holy apostles and prophets; for God hath avenged you on her. And a mighty angel took up a stone like a great millstone, and cast it into the sea, saying, Thus with violence shall that great city Babylon be thrown down, and shall be found no more at all.*

As you do fivefold ministry, ask God what principalities, territorial spirits, and powers will attack your vision. You can learn more about this in my book, *"Igniting Regional Revival."* In that book, I give revelation of how to discern principalities and powers and have an entire chapter on the character operations of these entities and how to thwart them. It is important to learn your enemy. Believe me, they are taking the time to learn you and your vision. The more you know about the strongholds that bind your region, the more effective you can be casting out the darkness and with releasing your vision. You will have revelation of how your vision will impact the region to reveal the light and kingdom of God. You will also know what is binding the people, the land, communities, and the atmosphere and are able to effectively plant, plow, and build despite warfare and challenges. God can give you revelation and insight on how to handle warfare and challenges and to displace darkness.

Though the enemy will want to believe you are not ready for these spheres or to plant and build vision, please know it is a lie. As God ignite you for fivefold ministry, the supernatural might of God will come upon you in and out of seasons to direct the vision.

> ***Isaiah 11:2-5*** *And the spirit of the Lord shall rest upon him, the spirit of wisdom and understanding, the spirit of counsel and might, the spirit of knowledge and of the fear of the Lord; And shall make him of quick understanding in the fear of the Lord: and he shall not judge after the sight of his eyes, neither reprove after the hearing of his ears: But with righteousness shall he judge the poor, and reprove with equity for the meek of the earth: and he shall smite the earth with*

*the rod of his mouth, and with the breath of his lips shall he slay the wicked. And righteousness shall be the girdle of his loins,
and faithfulness the girdle of his reins.*

Might is <u>*gebûrâ*</u> in Hebrew and means:
1. force (literally or figuratively); by implication, valor, victory
2. mastery, might, mighty (act, power), power, strength
3. bravery, mighty deeds (of God)

The spirit of wisdom, understanding, counsel, and the reverential fear SHIFTS boldly upon you; so, does the spirit of might.

Ephesians 3:16-21 *That he would grant you, according to the riches of his glory, to be strengthened with might by his Spirit in the inner man; That Christ may dwell in your hearts by faith; that ye, being rooted and grounded in love, May be able to comprehend with all saints what is the breadth, and length, and depth, and height; And to know the love of Christ, which passeth knowledge, that ye might be filled with all the fulness of God. Now unto him that is able to do exceeding abundantly above all that we ask or think, according to the power that worketh in us, Unto him be glory in the church by Christ Jesus throughout all ages, world without end. Amen.*

Might is <u>*dynamis* in Greek and means:</u>
1. force (literally or figuratively); specially, miraculous power (usually by implication a miracle itself)
2. ability, abundance, meaning, might (-ily, -y, -y deed)
3. (worker of) miracle(-s), power, strength, violence, mighty (wonderful) work, virtue
4. strength power, ability
    a. inherent power, power residing in a thing by virtue of its nature, or which a person or thing exerts and puts forth
    b. power for performing miracles
    c. moral power and excellence of soul
    d. the power and influence which belong to riches and wealth
    e. the power and influence which belong to riches and wealth
    f. power and resources arising from numbers
    g. power consisting in or resting upon armies, forces, hosts

The Spirit of might enables you to supernatural do what you could not do in your own strength. The spirit of might SHIFTS you into operating as a master builder.

***1Corinthians 3:10** According to the grace of God which is given unto me, as a wise masterbuilder, I have laid the foundation, and another buildeth thereon. But let every man take heed how he buildeth thereupon.*

The spirit of might comes through the Holy Ghost and enables you to function as the architect as well as the one who will construct, build, overthrow darkness, and deliver the region with kingdom authority and power. You must know this truth and convey it to demons, witches, people who are accustomed to talking you out of the vision. You are not doing this work alone or through your own means, but by the *dynamis* power of the Holy Ghost. This truth will release you from the fears and pressures that would come to murder your courage carry vision. I am joining with you in decreeing a limitless endowment of the spirit of might is your portion as you SHIFT forth in your fivefold vision. SHIFT!

Homework Explorations
1. Journal your thoughts concerning how principalities and powers attack vision carriers.
2. Journal your thoughts on the weapon of rest and how to be offensive against attacks.
3. Journal your thoughts and experiences on demonic night attacks.
4. Seek God for revelations regarding the principalities, territorial spirits, and powers that will attempt to attack your vision. Journal what he says.
5. Study the spirit of mighty. Spend time receiving the spirit of mighty from the Holy Spirit and asking him to endow you with it limitlessly. Journal your thoughts on the spirit of might being upon you to advance your vision.

Business & Fivefold Ministry

By: Elder Amanda Barnhill, Vision Carrier of Kingdom Shifters Ministries Muncie, Indiana

Visionaries and business activities within the marketplace come in innumerable forms such as stockbrokers, physicians, lawyers, entrepreneurs, farmers, Chief Executive Officers, Chief Financial Officer, Chief Operating Officer, teachers, plumbers, receptionist, cooks, etc. These various aspects of the business arena are vital to the advancement of the body of Christ within regions and spheres of influence. Apostle Paul and his partnership with Aquila and Pricilla is an example of the operation of the marketplace and ministry working together. In *Acts 18*, Apostle Paul was able to work with Aquila and Pricilla to generate income while he continued to work in Corinth and labor until the vision that God had given him was a success. Apostle Paul found Aquila and Pricilla to be versed in the things of God and having the ability to operate in business. The partnership worked because the foundation of both business and ministry is a servant's heart within the body of Christ. This positioned them to serve in a physical way as well as to minister within the marketplace, thus advancing the kingdom and spreading the Gospel and bring transformation to a region.

Acts 18:1-4 and 24-28 The Message Bible After Athens, Paul went to Corinth. That is where he discovered Aquila, a Jew born in Pontus, and his wife, Priscilla. They had just arrived from Italy, part of the general expulsion of Jews from Rome ordered by Claudius. Paul moved in with them, and they worked together at their common trade of tentmaking. But every Sabbath he was at the meeting place, doing his best to convince both Jews and Greeks about Jesus.

A man named Apollos came to Ephesus. He was a Jew, born in Alexandria, Egypt, and a terrific speaker, eloquent and powerful in his preaching of the Scriptures. He was well-educated in the way of the Master and fiery in his enthusiasm. Apollos was accurate in everything he taught about Jesus up to a point, but he only went as far as the baptism of John. He preached with power in the meeting place. When Priscilla and Aquila heard him, they took him aside and told him the rest of the story.

When Apollos decided to go on to Achaia province, his Ephesian friends gave their blessing and wrote a letter of recommendation for him, urging the disciples there to welcome him with open arms. The welcome paid off: Apollos turned out to be a great help to those who had become believers through God's immense generosity. He was particularly effective in public debate with the Jews as he brought out proof after convincing proof from the Scriptures that Jesus was in fact God's Messiah.

Marketplace ministers have a place within the body of Christ. When we separate the fivefold operations and the marketplace operations we reduce the status and influence of the marketplace ministers, thus depriving the fivefold team and the body of Christ from strategically being positioned as soldiers under the radar to closely see the operations of the enemy in our laws, educational systems, regions, and spheres of influence. We essentially are not aware of what is happening in these areas until decisions have been made and rooted within the region. We become reactive instead of proactive, which only makes complaints and not solutions.

2Corinthians 4:4 Amplified Bible among them the god of this world [Satan] has blinded the minds of the unbelieving to prevent them from seeing the illuminating light of the gospel of the glory of Christ, who is the image of God.

Ephesians 6:12 Amplified Bible For our struggle is not against flesh and blood [contending only with physical opponents], but against the rulers, against the powers, against the world forces of this [present] darkness, against the spiritual forces of wickedness in the heavenly (supernatural) places.

If the fivefold ministers and marketplace ministers partner there will be an equipping under the fivefold mandate for the work of the ministry within the marketplace, thus empowering the marketplace minister to walk in dominion and war with strategy against the things the enemy has erected within our jurisdictional governance.

Business and ministry work hand in hand in the Bible and were never intended to be separated but flow as one with the fivefold blueprint as the structure. Although *Ephesians 4:11-13* is a blueprint for fivefold ministry teams, it also shows that they are to equip the saints to walk in the fullness of destiny. It does not exclude the marketplace, businesses, or entrepreneurs, but in fact, the scripture says that the fivefold team is to build up and unify the body of Christ. As the fivefold ministers equip the body of Christ, those being equipped begin to take on the charter, nature, and God-given identity. This does not change just because one goes to work, or because of being an entrepreneur, but it should be consistent. *Ephesians 4:14* states that this fivefold structure is established so that the body of Christ will not be tossed to and fro or deceived. The enemy would love nothing more than for there to be a separation because it leaves the door open to receiving a measure and being deceived that we are operating in the fullness of the dominion that has been given to us as a kingdom heir. There is to be oneness and soundness to fivefold ministry and marketplace flow. This allows for us as a unit to expand, occupy, and recover. It also allows us to establish the kingdom and government of God as the standard for which our laws, land, educational systems, regions, and sphere of influences operate.

Ephesians 4:11-14 Amplified Bible (AMP) And [His gifts to the church were varied and] He Himself appointed some as apostles [special messengers, representatives], some as prophets [who speak a new message from God to the people], some as evangelists [who spread the good news of salvation], and some as pastors and teachers [to shepherd and guide and instruct], ¹² [and He did this] to fully equip and perfect the saints (God's people) for works of service, to build up the body of Christ [the church]; until we all reach oneness in the faith and in the knowledge of the Son of God, [growing spiritually] to become a mature believer, reaching to the measure of the fullness of Christ [manifesting His spiritual completeness and exercising our spiritual gifts in unity]. So that we are no longer children [spiritually immature], tossed back and forth [like ships on a stormy sea] and carried about by every wind of [shifting] doctrine, by the cunning and trickery of [unscrupulous] men, by the deceitful scheming of people ready to do anything [for personal profit].

Impacting economic and political arenas
Impacting our regions and sphere of influence in the economic and political arenas through the marketplace ministers and fivefold partnership is truly depending on the proper equipping of the marketplace ministers.

Dictionary.com defines *economy* as:
1. thrifty management; frugality in the expenditure or consumption of money, materials, etc.
2. an act or means of thrifty saving; a saving: the management of the resources of
3. a community, country, etc., especially with a view to its productivity
4. the prosperity or earnings of
5. the disposition or regulation of the parts or functions of any organic whole; an organized system or method
6. the efficient, sparing, or concise use of something
7. the divine plan for humanity, from creation through redemption to final beatitude
8. the method of divine administration, as at a particular time or for a particular race

Dictionary.com defines *economic* as*:*
1. pertaining to the production, distribution, and use of income, wealth, and commodities.
2. of or relating to the science of economics
3. pertaining to an economy, or system of organization or operation
4. especially of the process of production
5. involving or pertaining to one's personal resources of money:to give up a large house for economic reasons
6. pertaining to use as a resource in the economy: economic entomology; economic botany
7. affecting or apt to affect the welfare of material resources: weevils and other economic pests

To operate effectively in an economy where it impacts the distribution of wealth, income, and resources, and there is evident fruit, equipping in stewardship is vital. According to the US census bureau, the poverty rate for 2018 was 12.3% with a population of 327.16 million. Of the 327.16 million, only 33% of the population is reported as budgeting and stewarding their finances. This hinders the ability to truly have resources and have a say in the development of our regions and sphere of influence. The development of our regions, the betterment of our properties, and management of the distribution of funding(into our churches, our businesses, our school systems, etc.) starts with the empowerment and development of the character, identity, and destiny of those that are being sent into the marketplace. Because there has been a separation in the marketplace arena and the fivefold ministry, people are operating in the marketplace uncovered and ill-equipped and trained with certain biblical principles but a contaminated well. Being developed in character, identity, and destiny helps those in the marketplace to discern and bring strategy to the trainings they will take to equip them in their skill. The balance for kingdom and skill work hand in hand and need to flow together. Learning to become operable in this flow and dimension allows building of influence by becoming one of good report while exuding the standard of the kingdom of God.

The political arena impacts our laws, educational development, government, and parties.

According to dictionary.com *politics* means:
1. the science or art of political government
2. the practice or profession of conducting political affairs
3. political affairs
4. political methods or maneuver
5. political principles or opinions: We avoided discussion of religion and politics
6. use of intrigue or strategy in obtaining any position of power or control, as in business, university, etc.

Entry into the political arena for marketplace ministers is needed for the rulership of God to be operable. Political arenas have the stigma of being crooked in operations, so it is important for the solidification of identity of the marketplace ministers, so they are not easily deceived as *Ephesians 4* stated, but they go into the arena as those who govern and have dominion to impact change within their jurisdiction and sphere of influence.

Within the last year, I have personally had the opportunity to work behind the scenes with our local government candidates and officials. I have been blessed to be equipped and trained in my identity, destiny, character, nature, gifting, and calling within a fivefold ministry team. I have also been challenged by my team in areas in which I need to grow and develop as God begins to open the doors to business and government. As I have entered the political arena, I have been serving in small capacities, but the favor on my life opens up the doors to make greater connections in politics and the educational arena. With these opportunities, I have been able to go in with clear sight and see in the spirit realm in reference to my region and spheres of influence how the enemy has been operating. As our ministry team prays, we are praying as government officials of God to war in the spirit realm and nullify the operations that are not like God and establish his rulership in our region and spheres of influence. At the same time, in the natural when God gives me the opportunities to speak and share his heart for the region and his people, I do so with professional articulation from a place that they can understand, but with the authority of heaven backing me. I have learned before entering any meetings, lunches, or dinners to pray and fortify myself, and as I leave to cleanse. I have also learned my impact on the behavior, speech of others around me just by the stance that I take in the spirit realm. Often times, people may want to use certain language, and without saying a word they start to apologize for almost saying or thinking profane language or wanting to do something that they know is not part of my charter or nature. Although it may be a small beginning, it has opened my eyes in a new way to what God truly desires to do within government and the educational system and to have a heart to pray for a strategy for impact with what is in my hands.

Fivefold Structure within the marketplace

As fivefold ministries and marketplace operators, we have the standard of operating in both arenas, but our perspective on how to govern is different. Fivefold ministry teams is the structure for which true team operations should be modeled, even within the marketplace. Let's look at an organizational structure from the fivefold ministry team perspective.

President/CEO - This position in the organization is a vision caster. They often keep the organization focused on the purpose and truth of the vision. This position functions apostolically and establishes and plants the business and vision through strategy. They are goal setters, mission drivers, and value promoters.

Vision Strategist/Marketing/Financial Managers - This position is often looking ahead and seeing what is coming up the pike weather it is pitfalls, opportunities, etc. They analyze the situations and look for solutions. This position is prophetic. It is like a watchman on the wall sounding the alarm for what is coming.

Salesperson/Public Relations -This position spreads the word about the company and the good things about it in and outside the organization. This position operates like an Evangelist who shares the good news of Jesus Christ.

Trainers/Managers - This position takes the operations of the company and turn it into practical application. This position operates as a Teacher by equipping and bringing into maturity.
Coaches/Human Resources - This position has the heart to help people find their identities and strengths and find positions within the organization that will utilize the full potential of that. This position operates pastorally by shepherding the people.

When these areas work together within an organization, they function in a strong ability to overtake, expand, and grow in the market while economically advancing. Whether businesses, entrepreneurs, and marketplace operators know it or not, they operate within a type of structure aligned with the fivefold. Without fivefold ministries in place to train the true foundational areas of character, destiny, identity, nature, and calling then characteristics like greed and the spirit of mammon become intertwined within the structure that contaminates the fivefold blueprint within the business arena. We need fivefold business operations to develop and become the standard so that we can in turn continue to spread the word of God and transform lives that advanced the kingdom of God.

Unity opens the supernatural realms
The unifying of the fivefold and the marketplace produces the supernatural power to bring substance from the spiritual realm to the earth. It produces not only wealth but strategies and influence.

Deuteronomy 8:18 King James Version (KJV) But thou shalt remember the Lord thy God: for it is he that giveth thee power to get wealth, that he may establish his covenant which he sware unto thy fathers, as it is this day.

<u>Wealth</u> in Hebrew is chayil, khah'-yil and it means:

probably a force, whether of men, means or other resources; an army, wealth, virtue, valor, strength:—able, activity, ( ) army, band of men (soldiers), company, (great) forces, goods, host, might, power, riches, strength, strong, substance, train, ( ) valiant(-ly), valour, virtuous(-ly), war, worthy(-ily).

<u>Power in Hebrew is ko'-akh; or kôwach and it means:</u>
to be firm; vigor, literally (force, in a good or a bad sense) or figuratively (capacity, means, produce); also (from its hardiness) a large lizard:—ability, able, chameleon, force, fruits, might, power(-ful), strength, substance, wealth.

Supernatural power to get wealth gives the marketplace operators the ability to function as a chameleon which allows them to enter the marketplace and gain strategy while taking up territory and producing the truth and operations of God in the region and sphere of influence. Unifying brings the expanded capacity, strength, and boldness to pursue, overtake, and recover all while operating from the spirit realm and producing in the natural realm.

Without unity between fivefold and the marketplace, we are only operating in a measure and limiting the fruit that is to follow as kingdom heirs. True unification produces a oneness with a clear understanding that each part is working for the same vision and producing the success and mandate of the assignment. Unity is the source of power!

Unique Blueprint of Modern Evangelists

By Elder Mercedes Carr, Vision Carrier of Kingdom Shifters Ministries Muncie, Indiana

There are many ideas of what evangelism is and what it should look like in today's Church and society, but Jesus has given us the true blueprint for the evangelist. We can find Jesus giving us some of the most powerful examples of evangelism when we explore the gospels of Matthew, Mark, Luke, and John. The scriptures reveal that the evangelist was not only sent to preach but to help bring healing, transformation, and revival to the places they were assigned to. It was not uncommon for Jesus or one of the disciples to preach, teach, or release a word and miracles, signs, and wonders to follow. The evangelist often lays the foundation through the word and truth of God, opens the ground for revival and reformation to break forth in the earth, and in the lives of those who are present. Through their preaching they may break up the fallow ground in a region and bind the things that would hinder the people and region from receiving the fullness of what God wants to do in that place. This is why we must carry the word of God with us so that we are prepared to release it wherever God sends us. Being sent as an evangelist is key to your specific blueprint, calling, and assignments.

Luke 8:1 Soon afterwards, He began going around from one city and village to another, proclaiming and preaching the kingdom of God. The twelve were with Him.

Luke 4:18-19 The Spirit of the Lord is on me, because he has anointed me to proclaim good news to the poor. He has sent me to proclaim freedom for the prisoners and recovery of sight for the blind, to set the oppressed free, to proclaim the year of the Lords Favor.

Matthew 11:5 The blind receive sight, the lame walk, those who have leprosy are cleansed, the deaf hear, the dead are raised, and the good news is proclaimed to the poor.

There is an anointing that has been placed on the inside of the evangelist to proclaim the good news and to walk in the grace of being sent. Walking in my calling as a prophetic evangelist has been a journey that is constantly being built through faith and reliance on God. A prophetic evangelist is one who flows both in the prophetic and in the calling of the evangelist. I believe that everyone functioning in the fivefold ministry should have some insight and understanding of the prophetic, apostolic, teaching, preaching, and evangelistic anointing. Although God tends to flow through me in both the prophetic and evangelistic wells, the evangelistic anointing tends to be the well that I flow through more strongly.

Looking back on my life, I can identify the areas and experiences that God allowed to take place in order to awaken the calling of prophetic evangelism inside of me. When examining my upbringing and spiritual journey, I see that evangelism has always been one gift in the fivefold ministry that I identified with and embodied. Those who are called to be evangelist generally have a natural engrained desire to see God's people healed, set free, and delivered. Not only do they desire to help transform those in the body of Christ, they understand the importance of preaching and embodying God's Gospel and extending the message of salvation, repentance, forgiveness, grace, and redemption to the non-believer. I urge you to look over your own life and identify some of the areas that stand out. Ask God what gifts he was awakening and pulling out of you during that time. Our experiences, talents, gifts, and desires often align with our calling and purpose in life.

When God began to reveal these areas and show me the gift of evangelism that he was stirring inside of me, I quickly began to research renowned evangelist and their ministries. I wanted to know more about those who walked in the calling of the evangelist and those who did it well. Rather than seeking God for my own personal blueprint, I wanted to look to someone else to speak to who I was called to be as an evangelist. I quickly sparked a desire for the healing anointing of evangelist Kathryn Kuhlman embodied, and to experience the power to bring thousands of people into conversion and salvation like evangelist Reinhard Bonnke. I have found that it is great to be stirred by the anointing and preaching of other evangelists and even desire to flow in the miraculous, but we must fulfill these miracles and mandates through our own anointing, identity, and blueprint.

The evangelist must be careful about rejecting themselves due to the lack of focus and equipping of the evangelist in the body of Christ. The enemy would love to have you accept the lie that you are unnecessary and lack importance because at some point you may be the only connection and lifeline between that soul and Jesus. We must be delivered from spirits of rejection, spirits of fear, spirits of comparison, and any other attack that would keep us from walking in our unique identity. There is only one you and you must be living in the fullness of who God ordained you to be, so that you can be an effective minister in any fivefold office you hold and govern.

In this season of learning to navigate my own blueprint, it was my apostle who brought clarity to the truth that I could not find many evangelists that I identified with because God had written a specific blueprint just for me. I thank God for sending her to help equip me and train me up in the confidence of God concerning my calling and destiny. At this time, I had major difficulty finding those who were equipping, encouraging, and raising up the evangelist, but she consistently poured into my identity and affirmed what God said about me as his evangelist. Going deeper in relationship with God and seeking clarity and strategy concerning this blueprint would be a major key to walking in the fullness of my destiny and calling. God quickly showed me that my identity was not found in my office, but that my office would be birthed from my identity, which was in Christ Jesus.

Once we are rooted and grounded in the word, the nature, and the character of Christ, only then can we effectively walk in our office. The moment I began to make my calling my source of pride and validation God took me through a season where he stopped speaking to me as the evangelist and started speaking to me as his vessel, his servant, his leader, and his daughter. He had to strip me of the fulfillment and validation that I found in the title and build me back up to becoming his pure evangelist in the earth. The gifts of the Lord are without repentance, but he cares much more about your heart and character than he does about your titles and offices.

The truth is, it is not easy being a blueprint. It is hard work being a pioneer. It can be painful being a trailblazer. Often times, we look to others as an example so we do not have to put in the work and plow the areas that God has designed us to plow. He has uniquely designed each of us to go deeper than the generation before us, and we have allowed fear of failure and uncertainty to keep us boxed in. Many of us follow the blueprint of others so that we can live in the realm of "just in case."

"Just in case those in my life do not get saved from the blueprint God has given me, I will use another blueprint."

"Just in case the people do not receive my unique gift and style of evangelism, I will use someone else's style."

"Just in case my anointing does not carry me to the places God has designed for me to go, I will conform to religion rather than being transformed into the blueprint that God has mandated me to be."

In order to walk in a true evangelistic anointing, we must dismantle these thoughts and paradigms. We must be ready to be molded and shaped in any manner that God prefers to refine us for the call that is on our lives. We have gotten too comfortable with flaunting our gifts around the church and on social media when truly we do not know who we are in the fivefold we have adapted to someone else's blueprint.

Many people who are called as evangelist today are pioneers and trailblazers as well. We see the needs in our society, communities, churches, jobs, and marketplace, but we cannot quite see where we fit in. God is raising up evangelist with his heart who are not afraid to release the blueprint that has been uniquely designed by him and stamped with his approval to be sent out into the land. When the Lord called me to be an evangelist, he shared that I would be an evangelist to the homeless, the bound, the abused, the addicted, and to those I came in contact with wherever my feet tread. As an evangelist, you are literally taking up ground and territory for God wherever you go! When I allowed God to merge my education and career with his blueprint, I began to truly walk in evangelism as a lifestyle. Sometimes God will allow you to experience hands on training at your local church, your job, your household, and different places that you are already assigned in order to become further equipped in your personal calling as an evangelist.

We are in a season where many evangelists will receive dreams, revelations, and fresh downloads from God, but because they do not line up with what they have already seen in the earth, they dismiss and reject it. I believe that God is sending us into the hidden and desolate places! He is sending us into the marketplace and the businesses! He has placed us in the shelters and the social service agencies to be agents of change. We will preach the gospel on our job and our coworkers will be saved! We will spread Gods good news in the grocery store and our neighbors and neighborhoods will be changed. We will release a word at the hospital and the sick will be healed just as the dead will be raised. This is Gods blueprint for us! We were not called to conform to a pulpit but made to be thrusted out as his change agents in the earth. SHIFT!

Homework Explorations

What questions do you need to ask God in order to gain greater clarity concerning his blueprint for your destiny?

In what areas do you need healing or deliverance in your identity in order to walk boldly in your purpose as an evangelist?

What spirits have come against your personal calling and destiny as it pertains to walking in your purpose as an evangelist?

In what areas do you need to further connect to other members in the fivefold ministry to grow as an evangelist?

Evangelists Working in Fivefold Ministry

The evangelist is an intricate part of the fivefold ministry that has been left out of many of the conversations, conferences, and strategies today surrounding the subject.

Ephesians 4:11-13 And He Himself gave some to be apostles, some prophets, some evangelists, and some pastors and teachers, or the equipping of the saints for the work of ministry, for the [edifying of the body of Christ, till we all come to the unity of the faith and of the knowledge of the Son of God, to a perfect man, to the measure of the stature of the fullness of Christ;

Everyone cannot be the prophet or the apostle. We all must play the part that God designed for us in order to be effective in the edifying and equipping of the saints. There are many ministries that are aiming to walk in the fivefold paradigm but have left behind the evangelist. There are some who are strong in the prophetic but are lacking teaching and sound preaching. There are those who are apostolic builders, but they have forgotten about the importance of the pastor. We need every element of the fivefold to function properly.

The evangelist can and should partner with each member of the fivefold ministry. While the evangelist may be the one who is bringing in the souls, we might work with the pastor and the teacher to help disciple those new members. While we may be the ones to initially preach the word that summons the people to God, we may partner with the apostle to discover the giftings and callings of that believer and help them adequately flow in building and expanding that which the Lord has placed on the inside of them. Although the evangelist may be the team member that desires to spend more time fellowshipping and socializing to draw in others and build relationship, each team of the fivefold should have some desire to connect with those seeking relationship with Christ, and a place to grow in their faith.

The evangelist has the tendency to move from one assignment to the next quickly and is always seeking new strategies and ideas to reach the lost and bound. If they are not careful, they will struggle to stay focused on a person or thing long enough to bring forth the resources needed for that person to reach true transformation. The evangelist is generally concerned with bringing as many people to God as possible. The apostle may come in and help instill balance to these areas where they are not just focused on quantity, but the quality of the relationships they are building. The apostle may help the Evangelist take one of the many ideas they have been strategizing about and encourage them to formulate a blueprint and expand that idea into a ministry or whatever God is saying at the time.

Although the evangelist may be the main person arranging fellowships and evangelism activities, they should also be helping to develop and activate a culture of evangelism in the fivefold team and the body of Christ as a whole. Each team member should be concerned about the souls and salvation of those in their community and region. The evangelist should be fervent in prayer and open to taking on the burden of laboring and warring for these souls. The evangelist should be praying with strategy to make sure the ground is not hard when the rest of the team is trying to impart into the region and the people who are attached to it. The evangelist's job does not stop once the people arrive to the event or church, they must continue evangelizing and stirring up the gift of preaching, exhorting, and encouraging, as a foundational part of the ministry.

I have observed a special anointing that breaks forth when the prophet and the evangelist partner together in ministry. The prophet has the ability to be the eyes and the mouthpiece of God, while the evangelist may feel the burden and the heart of God for the people who they are evangelizing to in that time. In that moment the evangelist might take the time to share a personal testimony that opens up the person to a new level of vulnerability, and the prophet can come in and impart a word once that trust has been established and blockages are down. The ministry that I am apart of tends to use the two by two method where two people will go together while evangelizing. We work with one another's gifts to truly release the mandate and assignment of God during that time. This method also brings protection and fortification to those who are ministering and being ministered to.

The evangelist ability to stay connected every member in the fivefold is critical. Evangelist can get so overwhelmed with souls and working with a multitude of people one on one, that they forget to plug back into their team and pour into those within their base. It is important for the evangelist to remain consistent in the assignments that God has given them in their home church, community, and region, along with the endeavors that they take on in regions outside of their own.

Do not grow weary in well doing. Pray that God gives you a team that can honor and help govern your gift and calling as an evangelist while you do the same for your team members. Evangelism is not an old practice or strategy. God is raising up his evangelist in this hour who know who they are and are ready to bring true and lasting revival, reformation, and transformation to our nation and the world at large. Focus forward, receive healing and deliverance in the areas that keep you from being an effective team member, and always stick to Gods blueprint. I charge you to arise and go forth in excellence, purity, and the heart of God as his evangelist in the earth.

Homework Explorations
1. Explore and journal the role of an evangelist in fivefold ministry.
2. Journal how your destiny and calling would work in ministry with an evangelist.
3. List ten ways you and your vision can evangelize in your community and region. Write three goals for at least five of the evangelism options on your list.

FIVEFOLD GLORY CHARGE!

From the Prophets of Kingdom Shifters Ministries

I prophecy greater glory is coming upon every saint. I prophecy a SHIFTING glory that transforms lives and destinies. I prophecies floods and floods of glory outpouring from heaven and being unveiled from the glory that is already been instill in and around the earth, for the word says, the earth is full of God's glory. I prophecy SHIFTING winds of glory blowing in every region, in every nation, in every home, in every life, in every family, in every generation. I prophecy the prosperity and riches of the glory being tangible and physically manifesting as glory is revealed and blow. I prophecy ever increasing glory as we go from destiny to destiny and glory to glory in Jesus. I prophecy deeper authoritative eternal glory that makes us well and whole as we continuously journey in covenant with the ultimate glory carrier - our Lord and Savior Jesus!

As you unlock and open deeper authoritative eternal glory that makes us well and whole, I prophesy it shall increase from generation to generation. I prophesy generational covenants shall be our portion as our children, children's children, and so on will worship you Lord in spirit and in truth. I prophesy the glory will be upon us so strong as we build in this season that we our capacity stretches beyond what we are used to. I prophesy you are breaking the spiritual dams where your glory cannot be contained in this season! I prophesy the glory is BREAKING BREAKING BREAKING BREAKING OUT NOW!

Jesus is our glory and our hope of eternal salvation and I prophesy we are SHIFTING greater and greater into his image and into his likeness as we behold him. I prophesy that his wings of glory are causing us to soar higher and higher as we release to him the cares and weights of this world. I prophesy healing glory over us all wherever we need his healing glory to flow. I prophesy wind after wind will carry us and lift us higher into the eternal plans of his glory. I prophesy the unity of his glory is SHIFTING each of us into greater communion with him and with each other. I prophesy the covenant of his glory is binding our hearts together in love and fellowship more and more each day.

I prophecy glory coming upon and eternally radiating from every fivefold vision. I prophecy that the revival fires will never burn out. That an igniting will contagiously consume every region with miracles, signs, and wonders, as the saints are trained, equipped, and releasing their fivefold visions in the earth. I prophecy where will be no ministry walls as the believers of God take over regions, infiltrate systems, and establish godly mountains for God's glory. I prophecy living a daily lifestyle of destiny will become the norm as saints create a culture that living for God is the only fulfilled way and demonstrate his kingdom in every area of their lives. SHIFT!

Resources

- *Apostolic Mantle by Taquetta Baker*
- *Blueletterbible.com*
- *Biblestudytools.com*
- *Dictionary.com*
- *Kingdom Decrees for Sustaining the Vision by Taquetta Baker*
- *Olivetree.com*
- *Pastoral Statistics Provided by The Fuller Institute, George Barna, Lifeway, Schaeffer Institute of Leadership Development, and Pastoral Care Inc. (https://www.pastoralcareinc.com/statistics/)*
- *Strong's Exhaustive Bible Concordance Online Bible Study Tools*
- *Sustaining the Vision Workbook by Taquetta Baker*
- *The US Army News & Information website (https://www.army.mil)*
- *Wikipedia*
- *Cover photo by Reenita Keys. Connect with her via Facebook.*

Contributing writes of the Fivefold Operations manuals.

www.ingramcontent.com/pod-product-compliance
Lightning Source LLC
Chambersburg PA
CBHW080405170426
43193CB00016B/2821